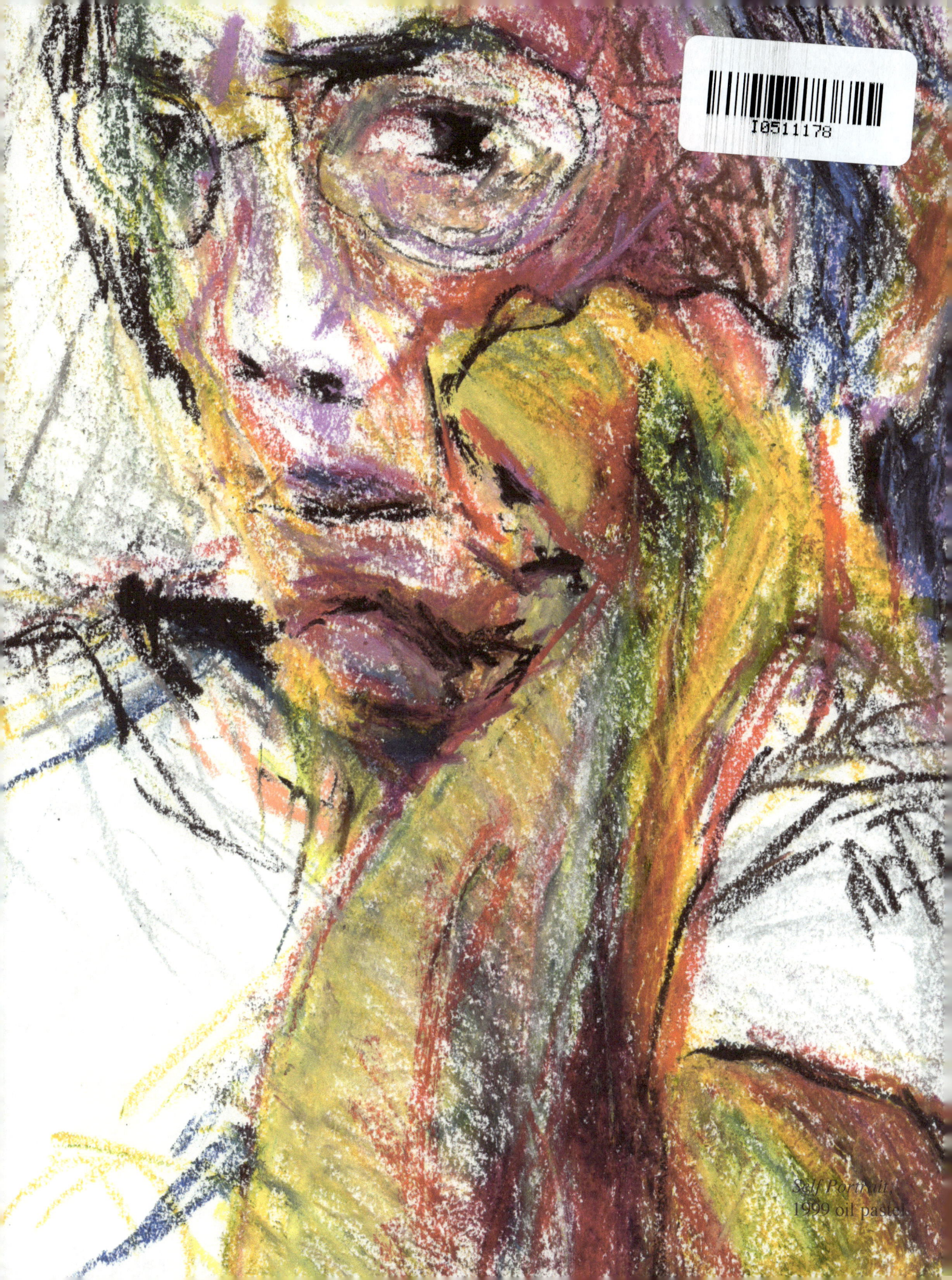

Self Portrait
1999 oil pastel

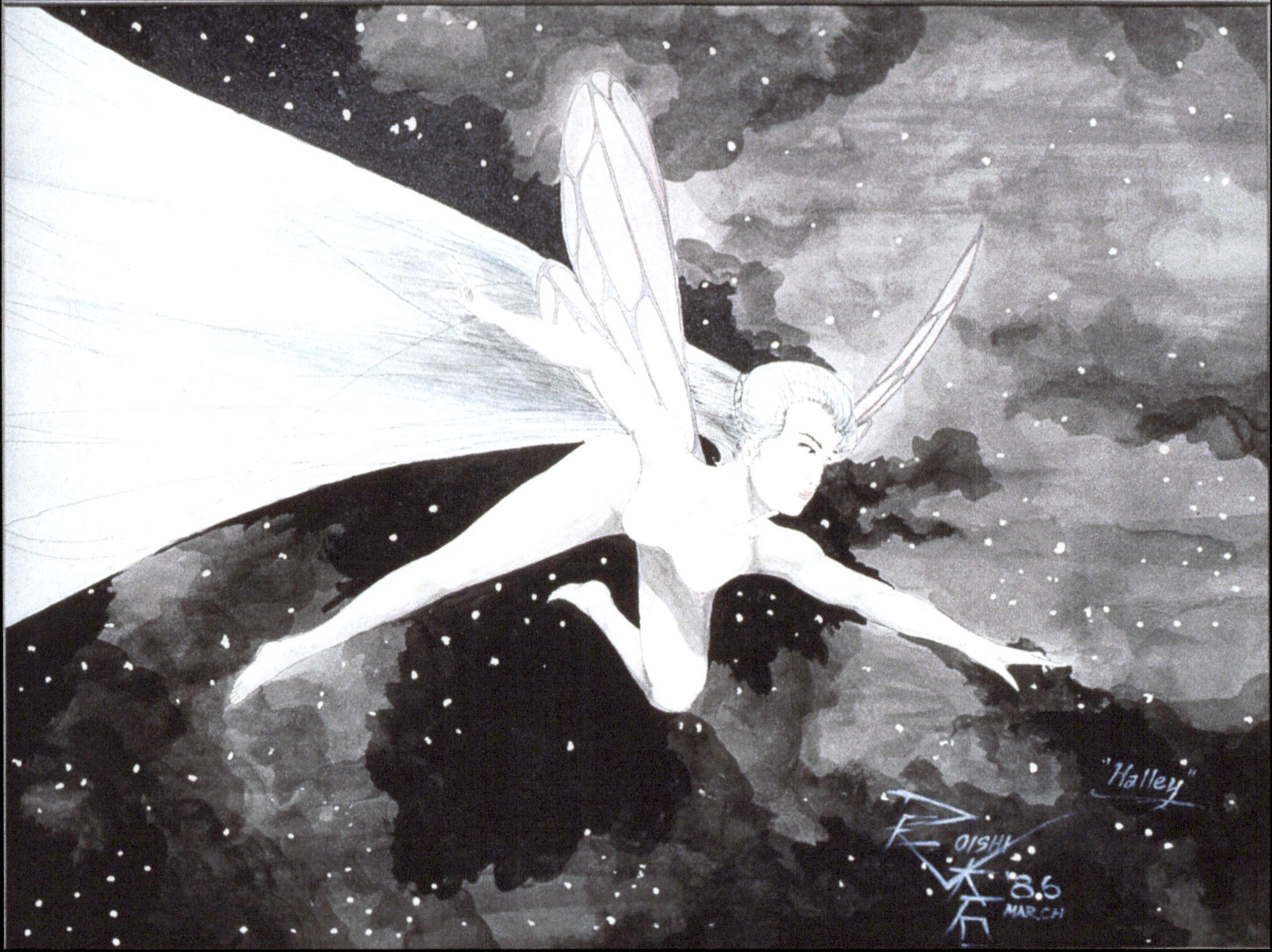

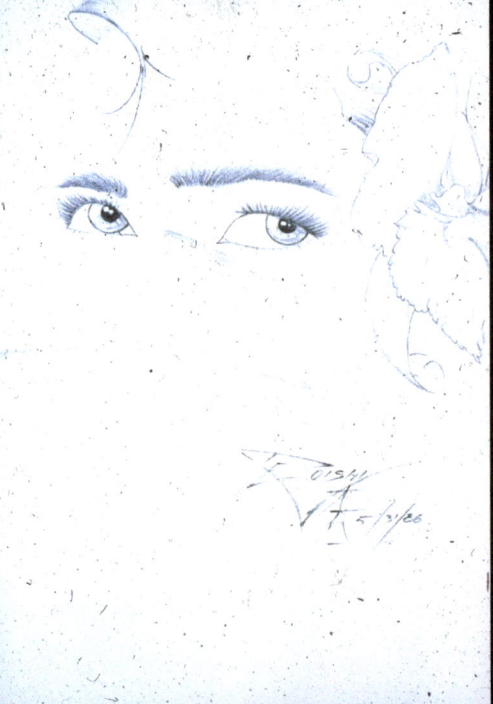

These two pages are images from high
school. I used them for my college
application.

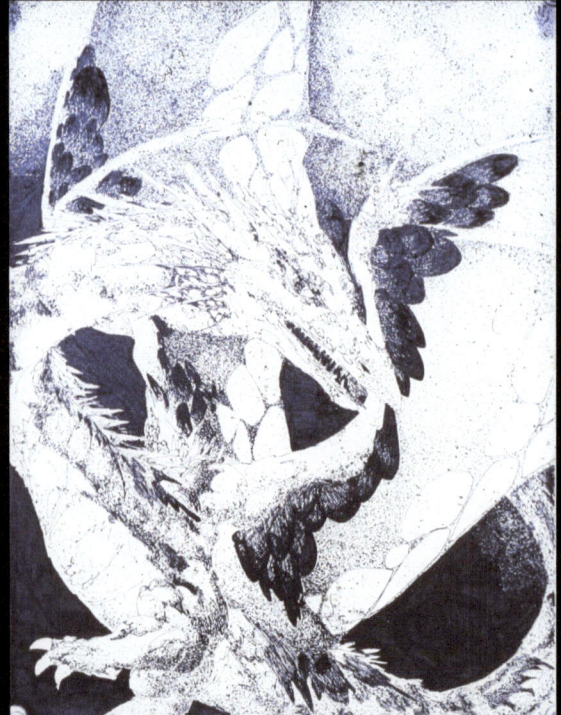

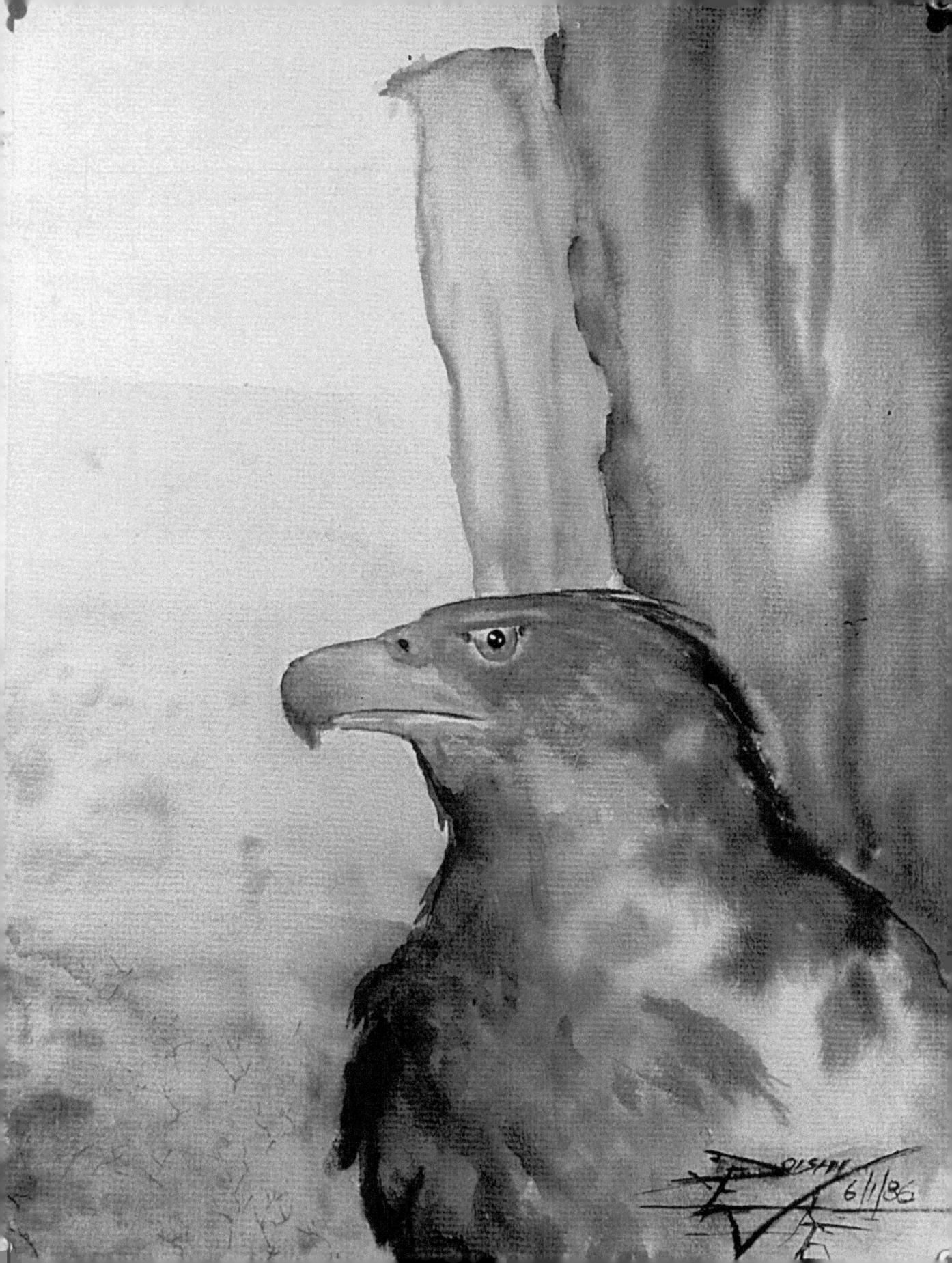

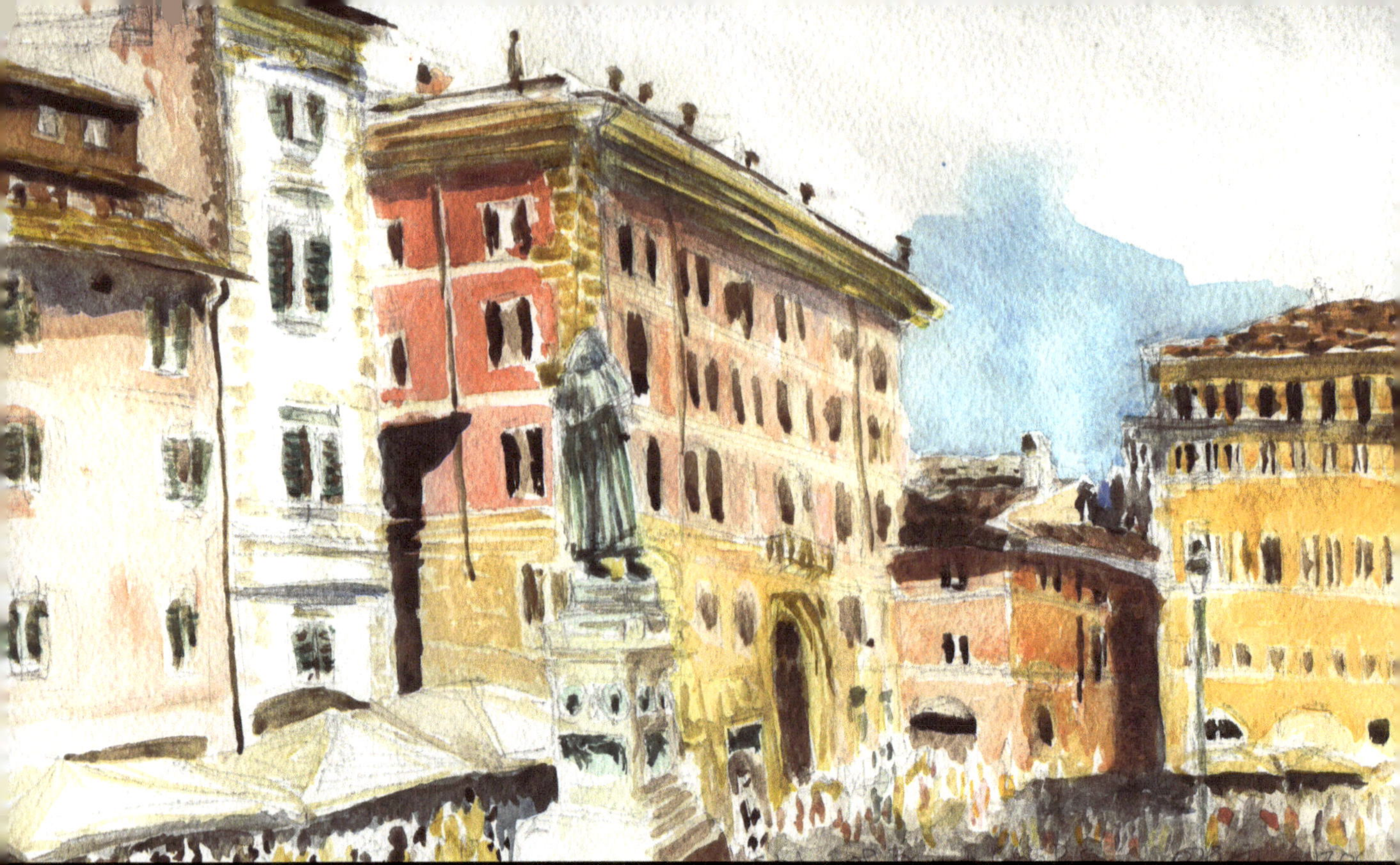

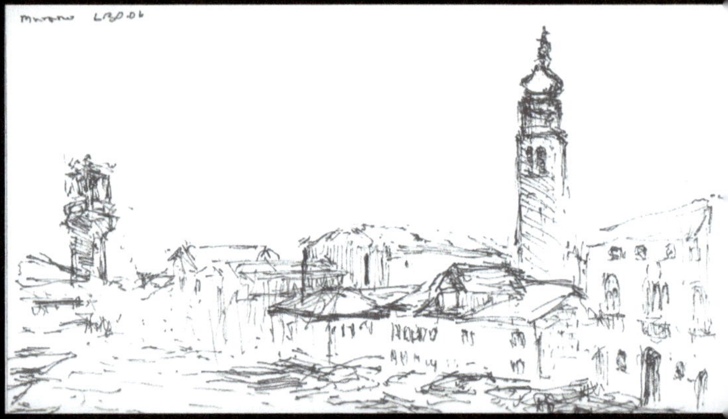

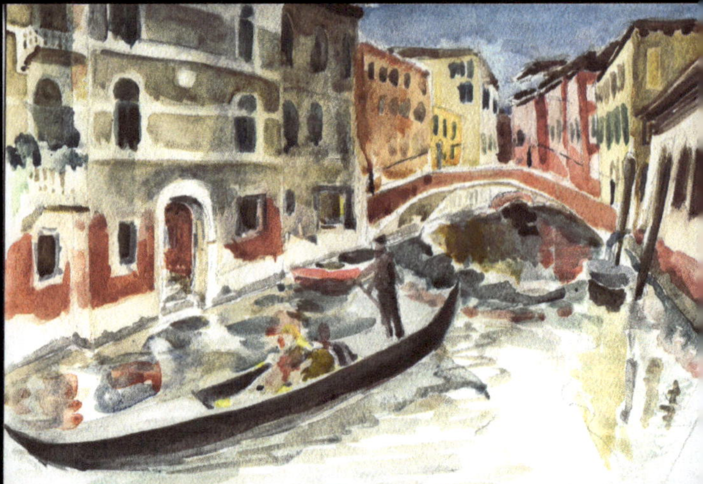

Murano L.3006

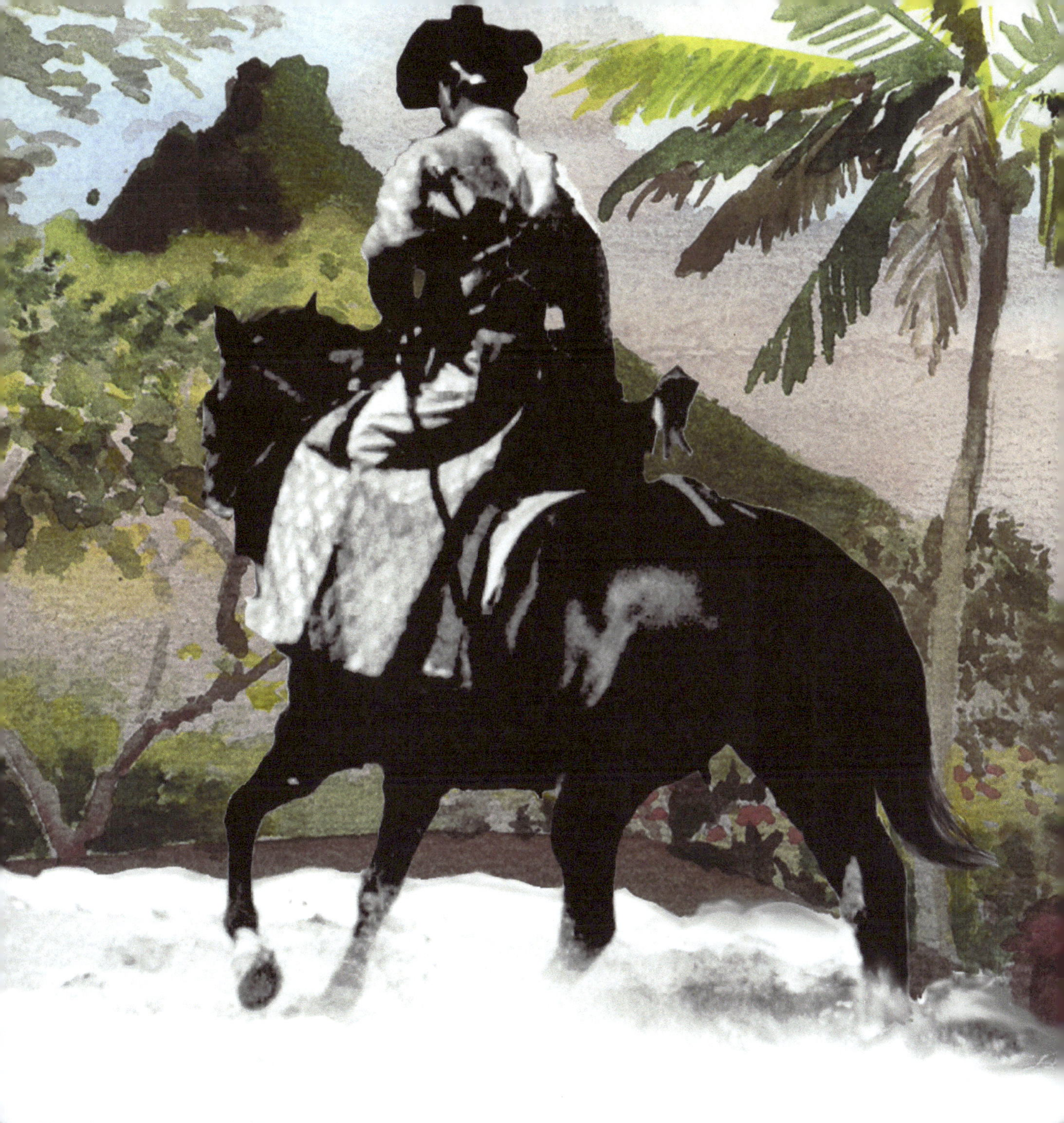

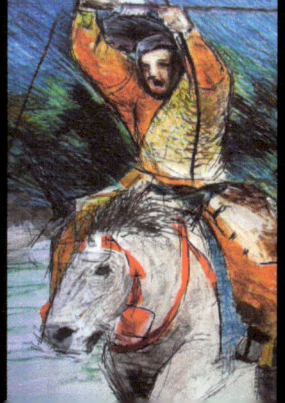

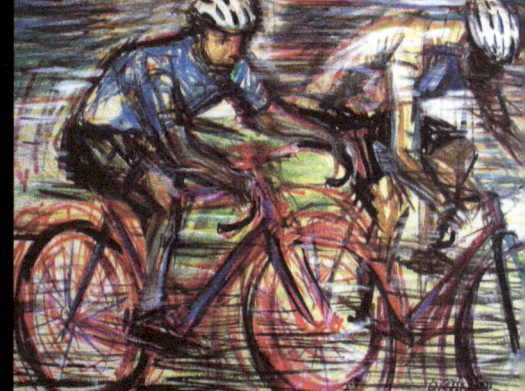

Campo De' Fiori, Roma, Italia, 2006,
watercolor
Murano, 2006, ink
Venice, 2006, watercolor
Sistine Chapel, 2006, ink

Yabusame, 2000 multi-media collage of
photo and watercolor (1st piece exhibited
at Honolulu Academy of Arts)
Kaneohe Criterium, 2001, oil on panel
Yabusame Charge, oil pastel

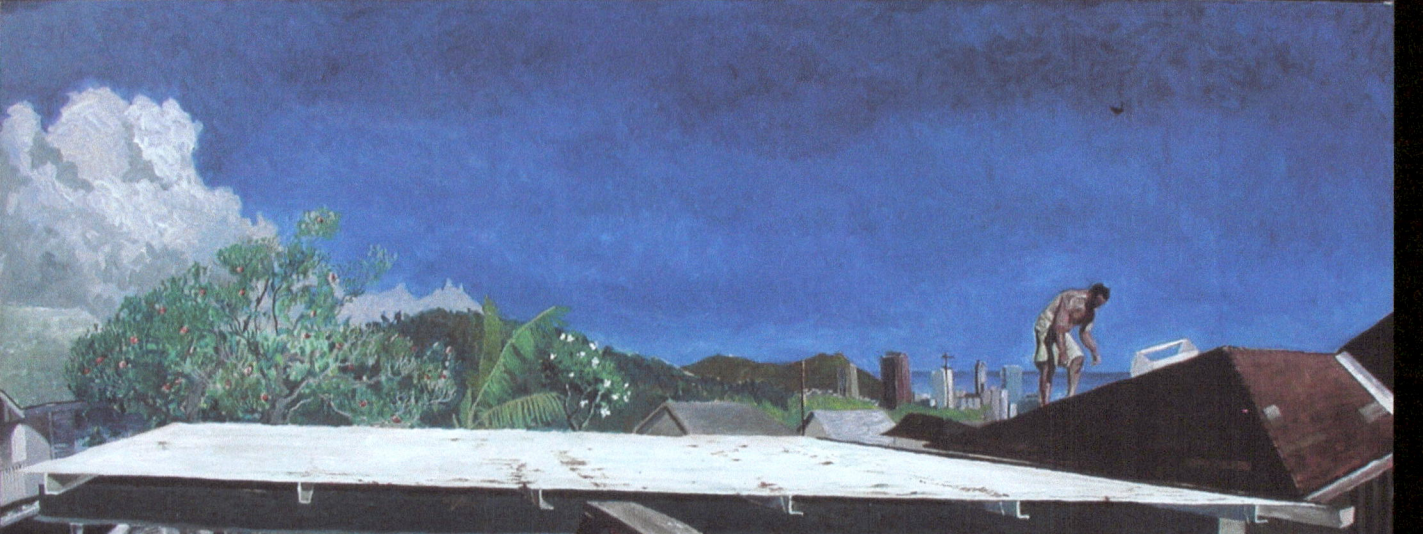

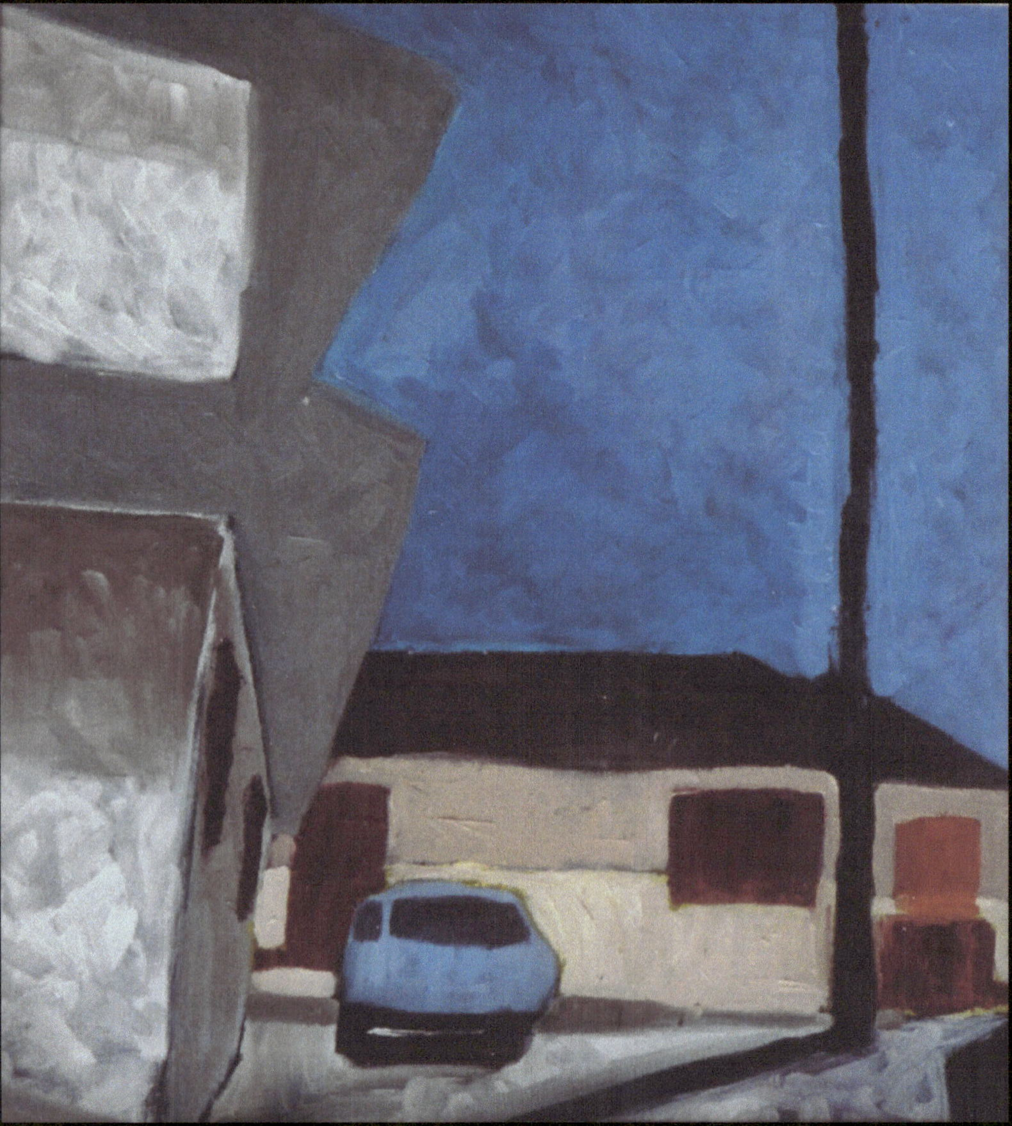

Working On the Roof: A Fine Day, 2000, oil on panel (2nd piece exhibited at Honolulu Academy of Arts)

A Fine Day: Neighbor's House, 1997, oil on canvas

Next Page:

Working On the Roof: A Fine Day (View From the Top), 2001, oil on panel

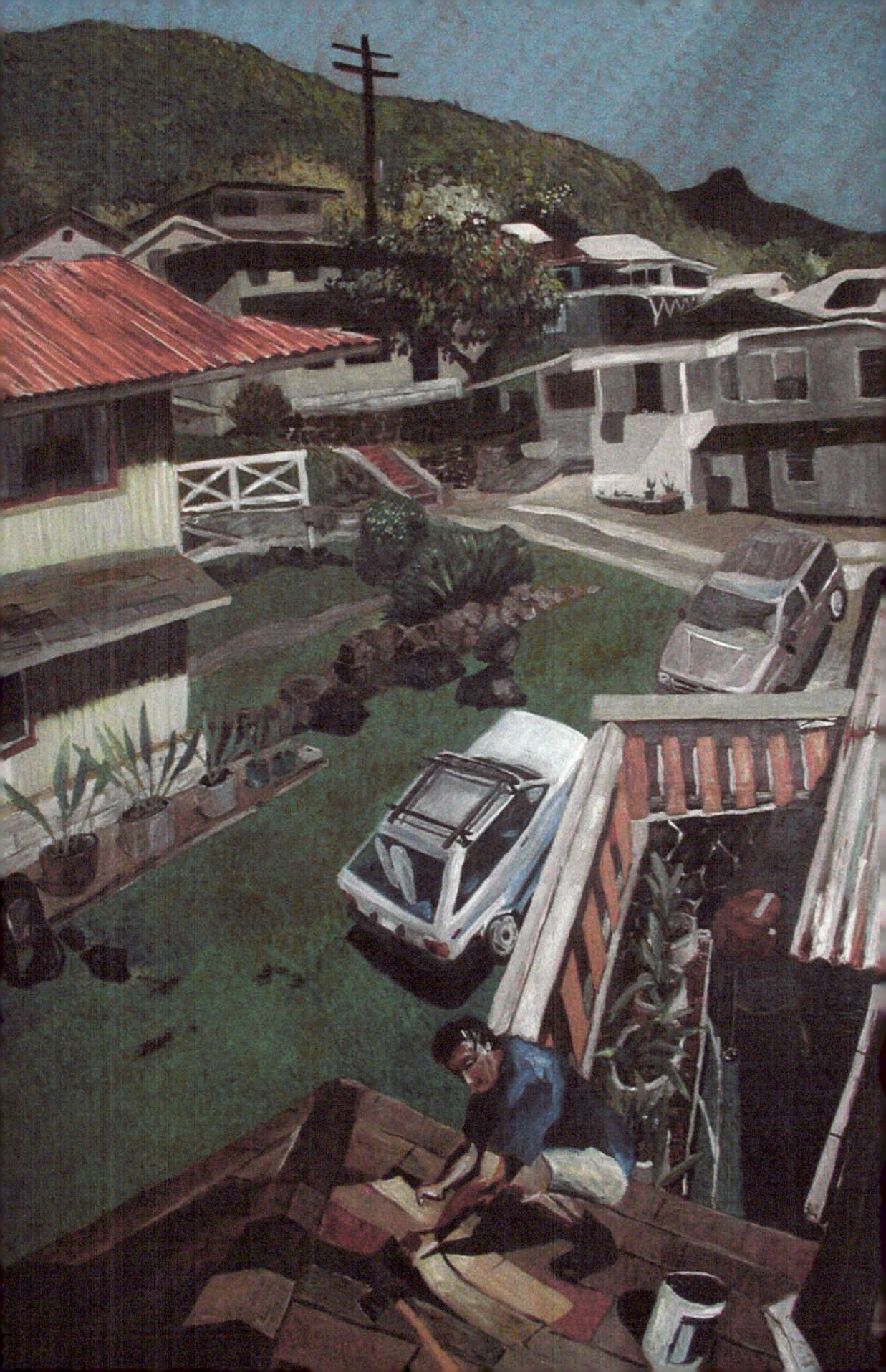

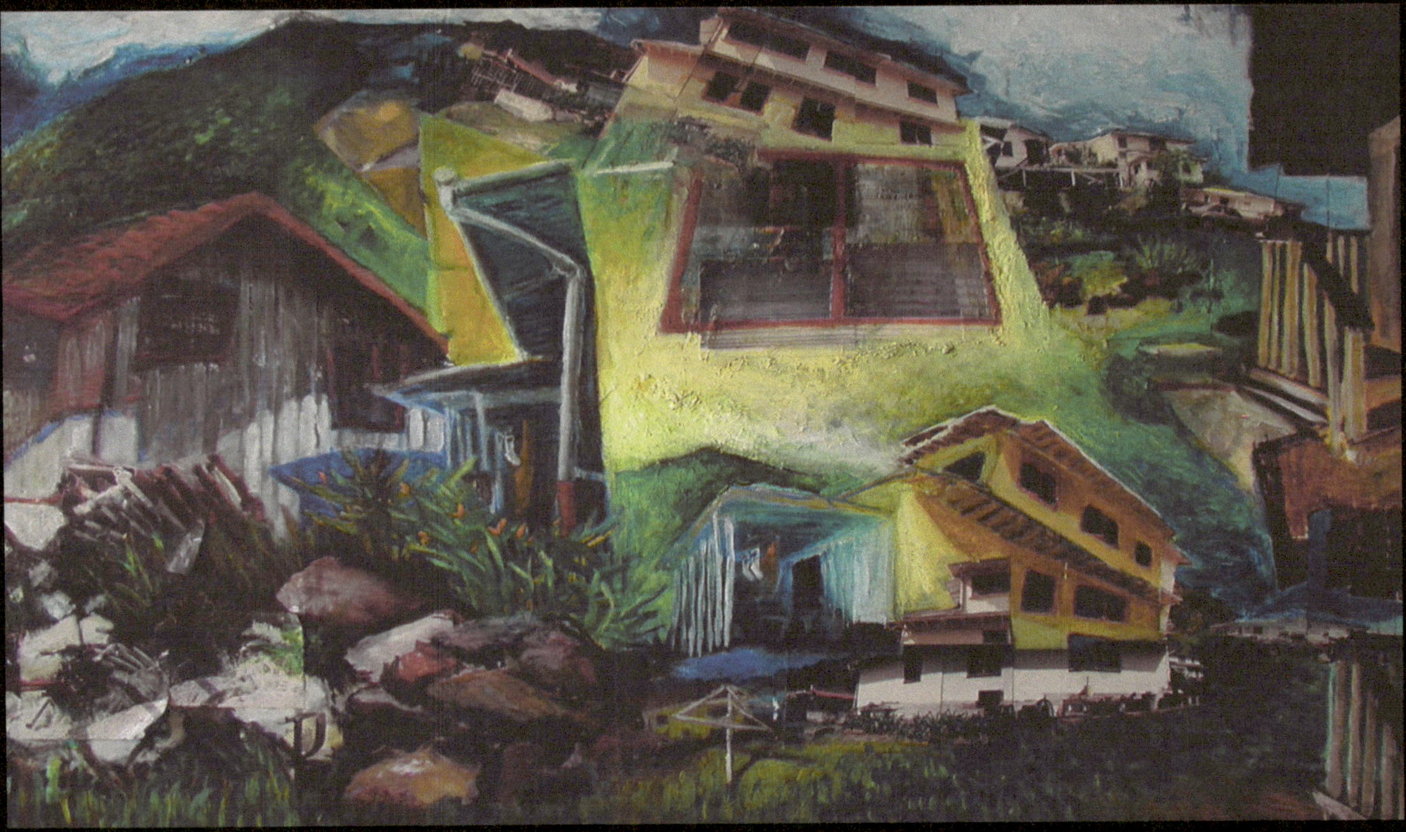

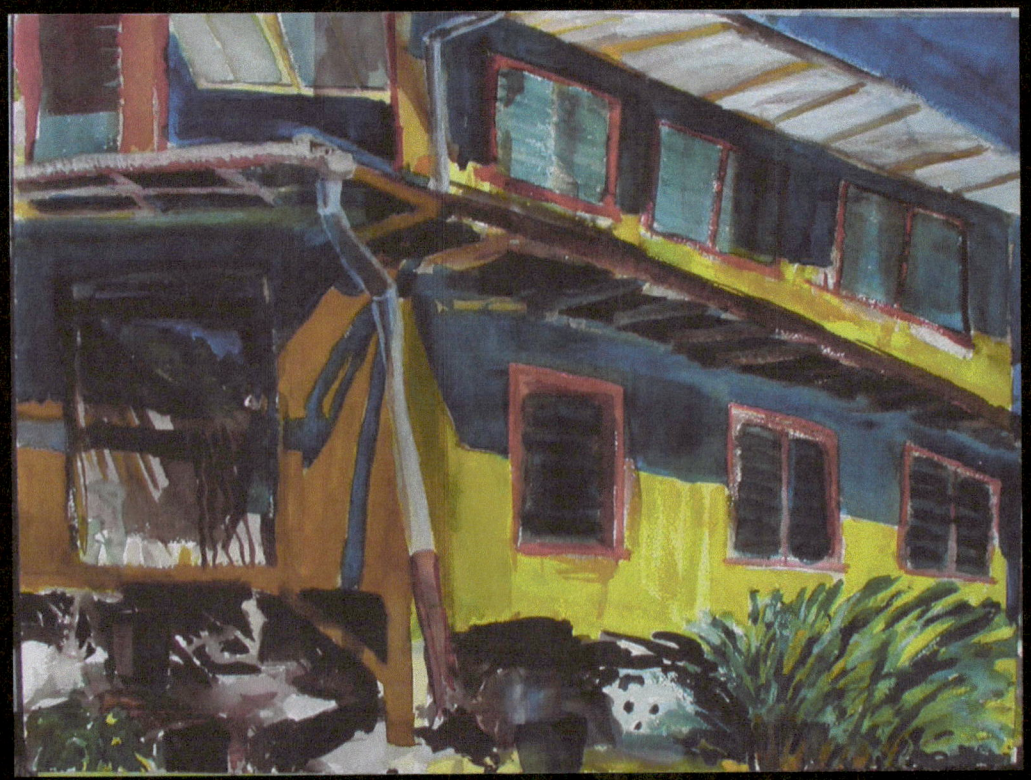

Grandma's House,
1992, acrylic, ink,
pencil, oil, encaustic,
and photo on panel
(Persis Collection
Award at Honolulu
Printmakers Exhibit)

*Grandma's House
(3/4 view),* water-
color

Next Page:

*The Light Embraced
the Window,*
1991, oil on canvas

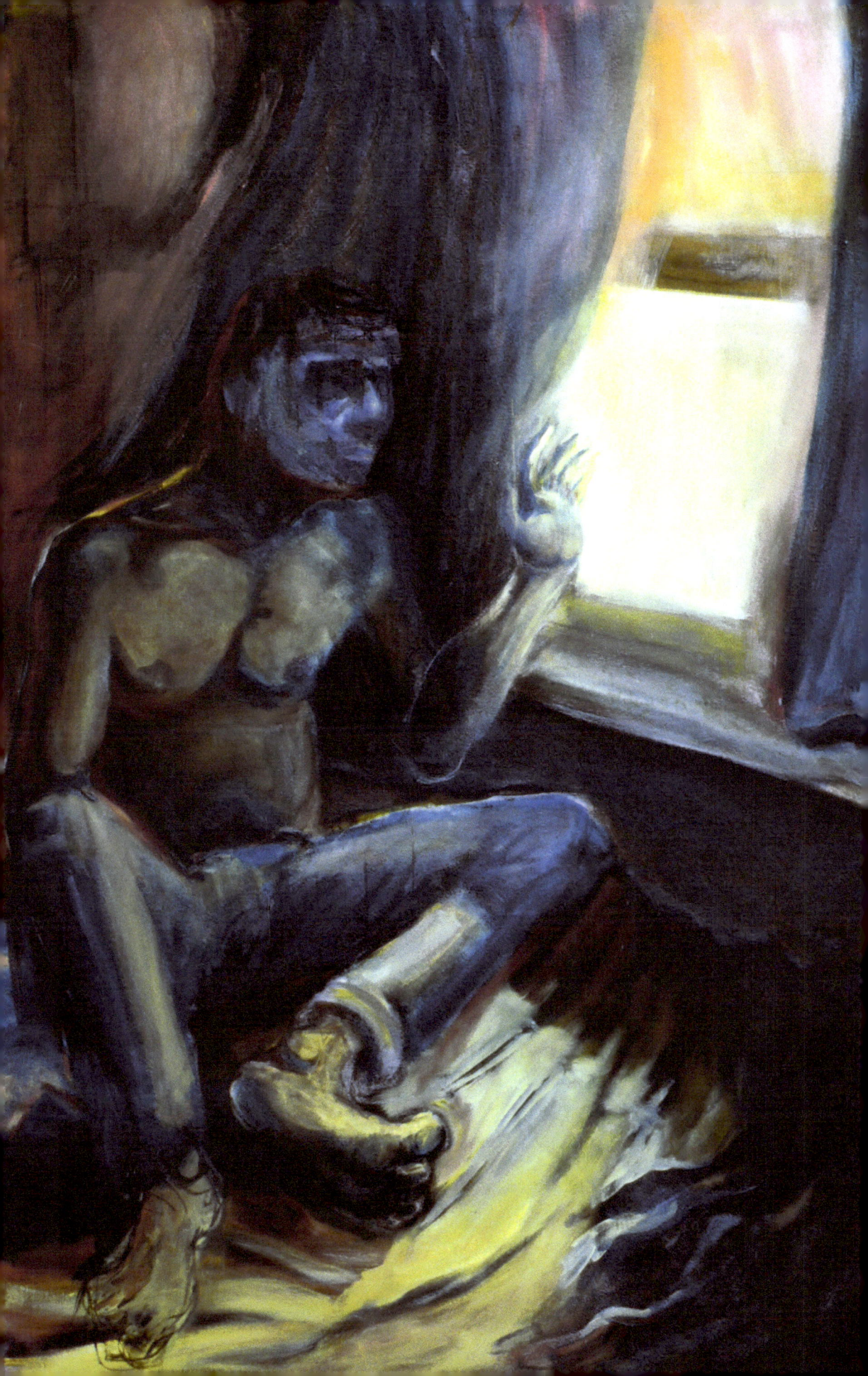

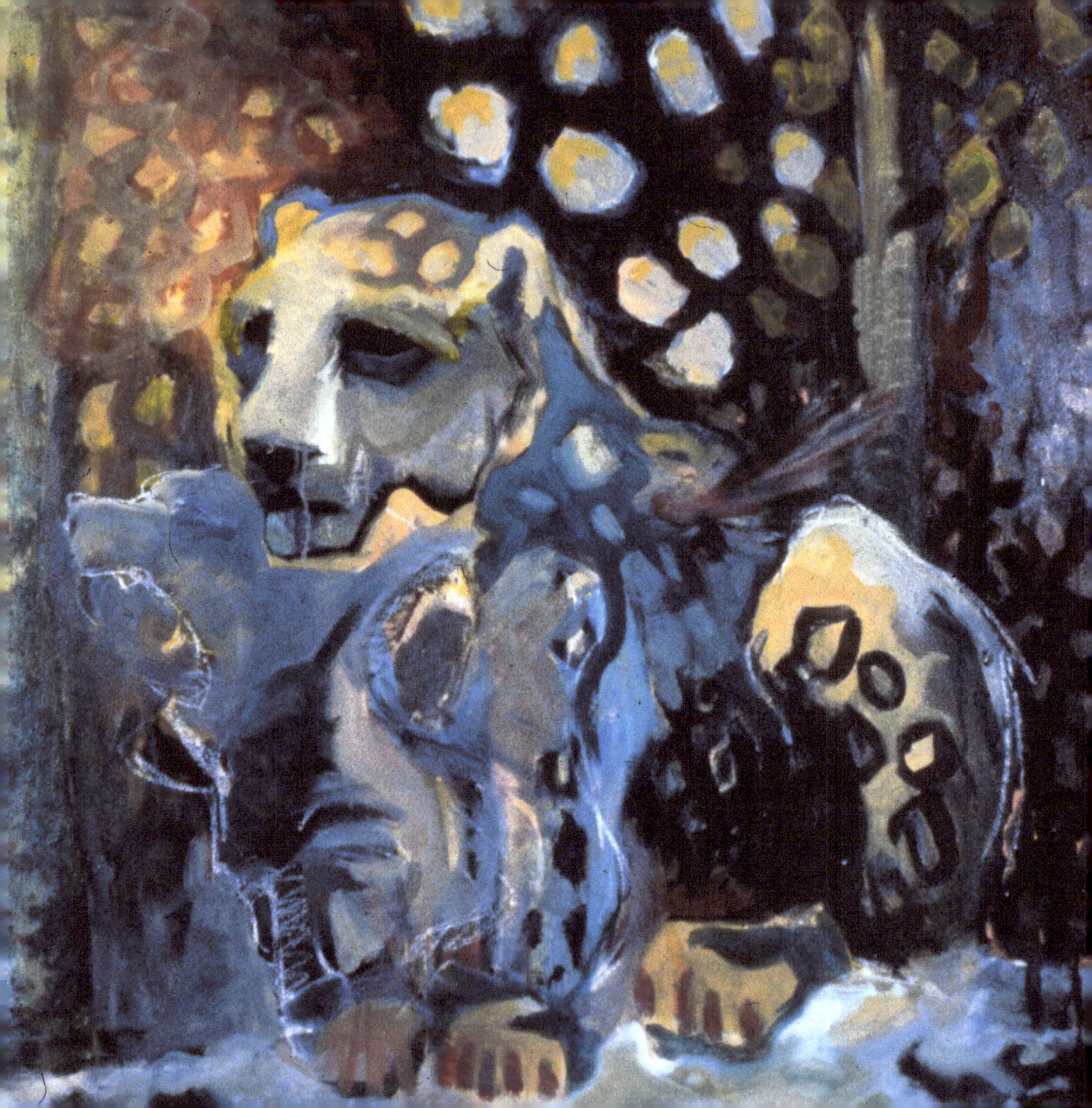

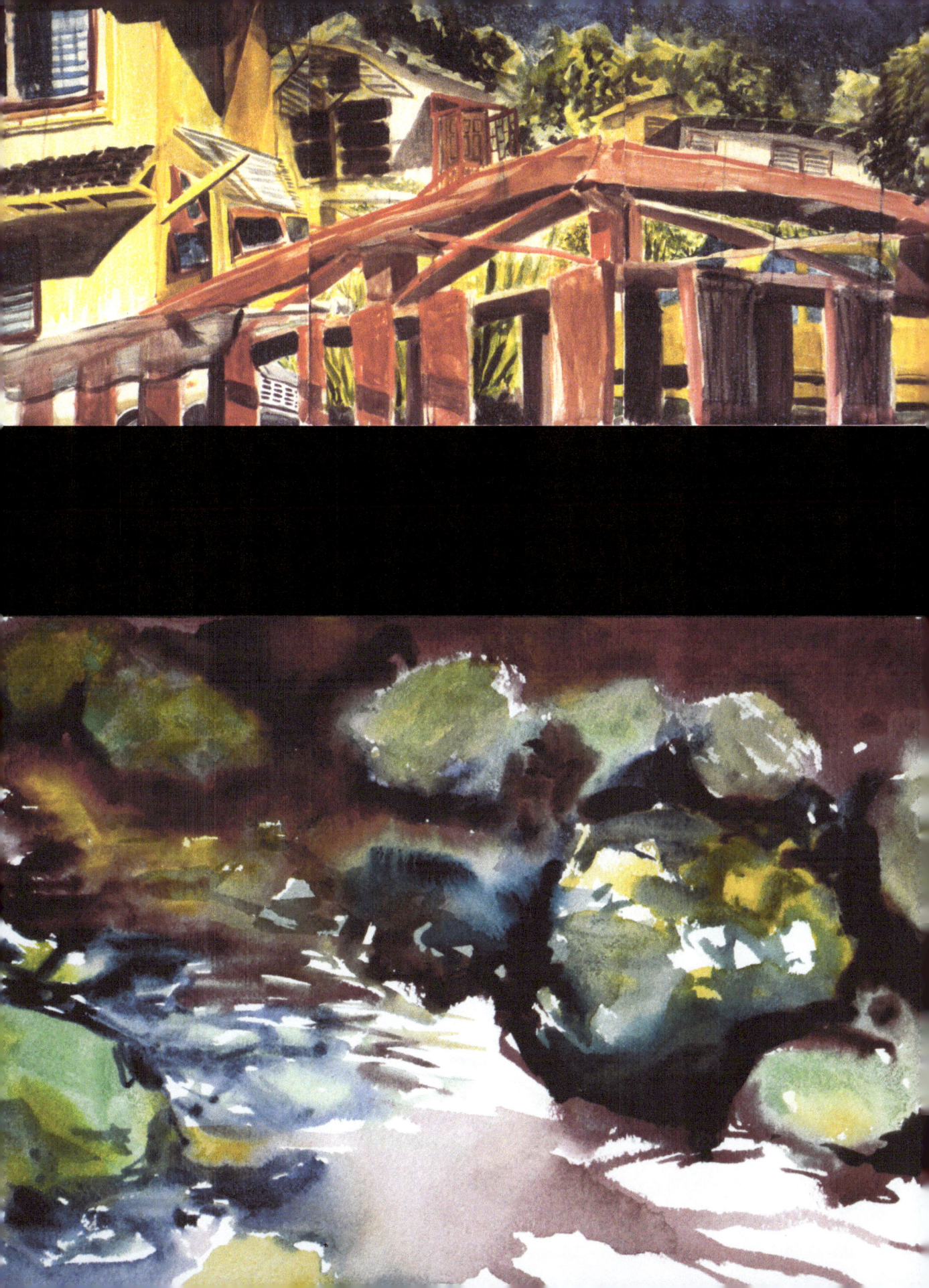

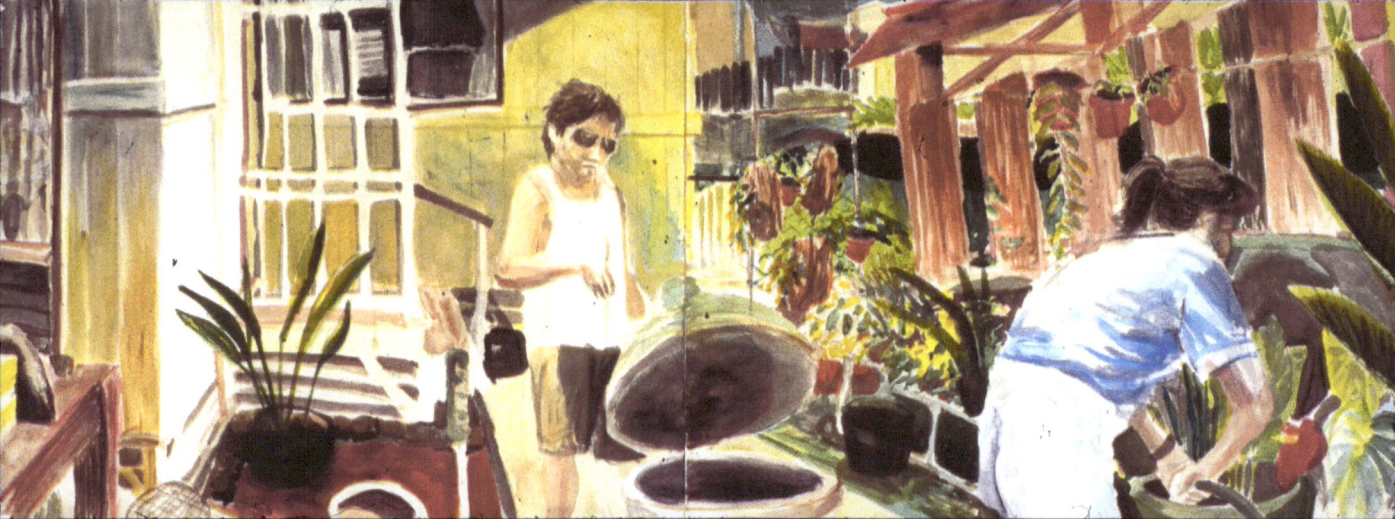

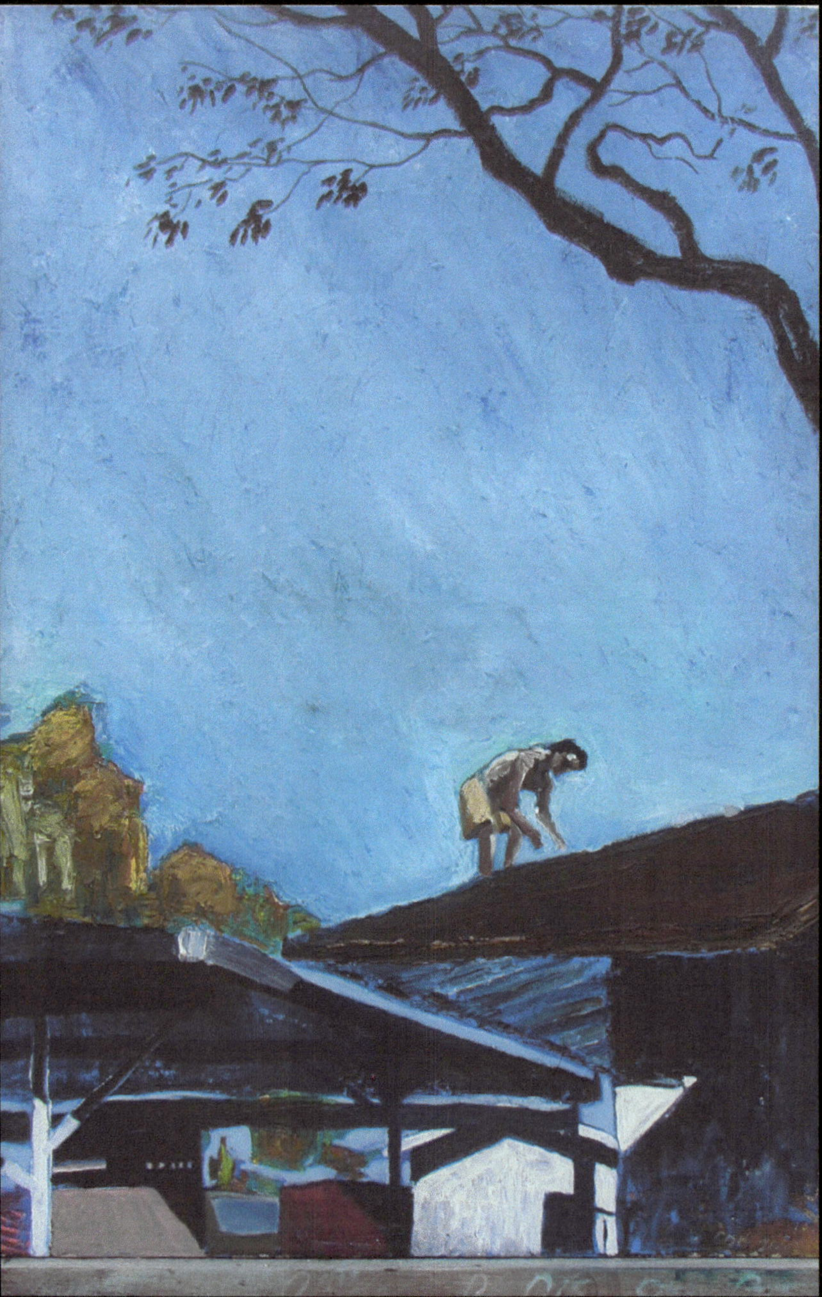

Brother Cooking, Mom Gardening, 1995, watercolor

Working On the Roof: A Fine Day, 2000-2003, oil on canvas

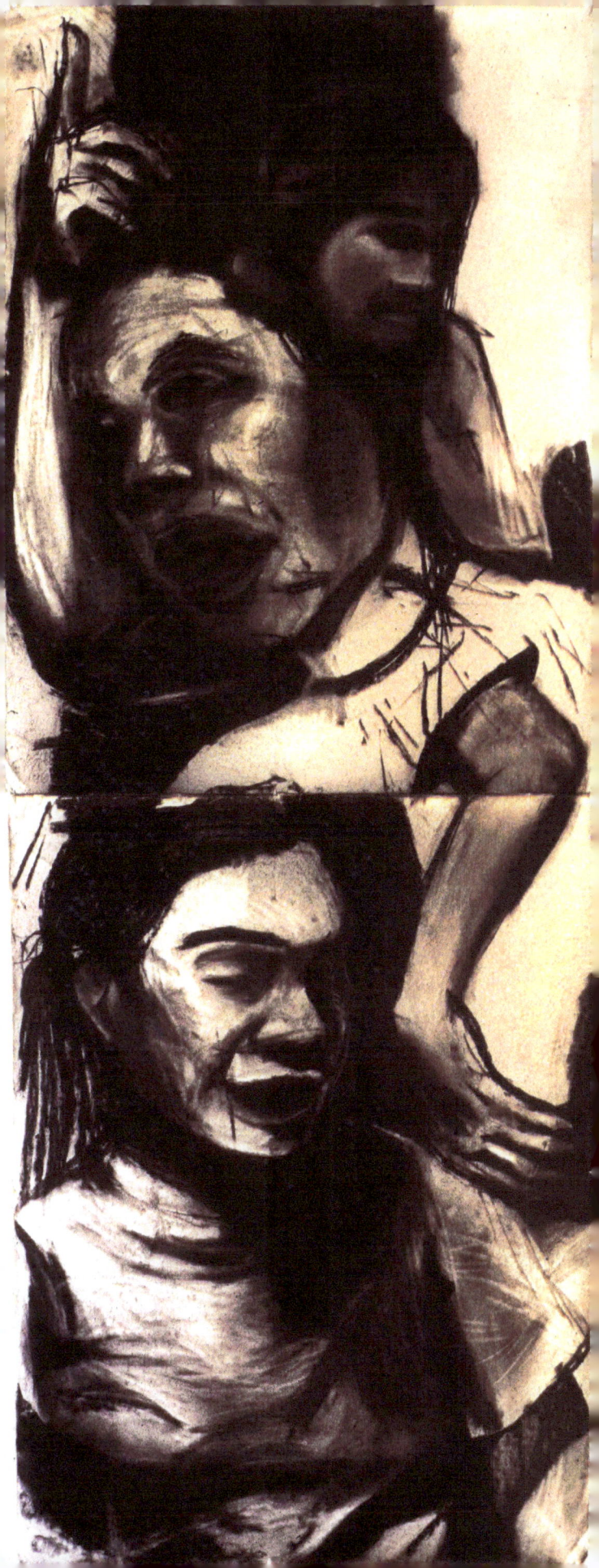

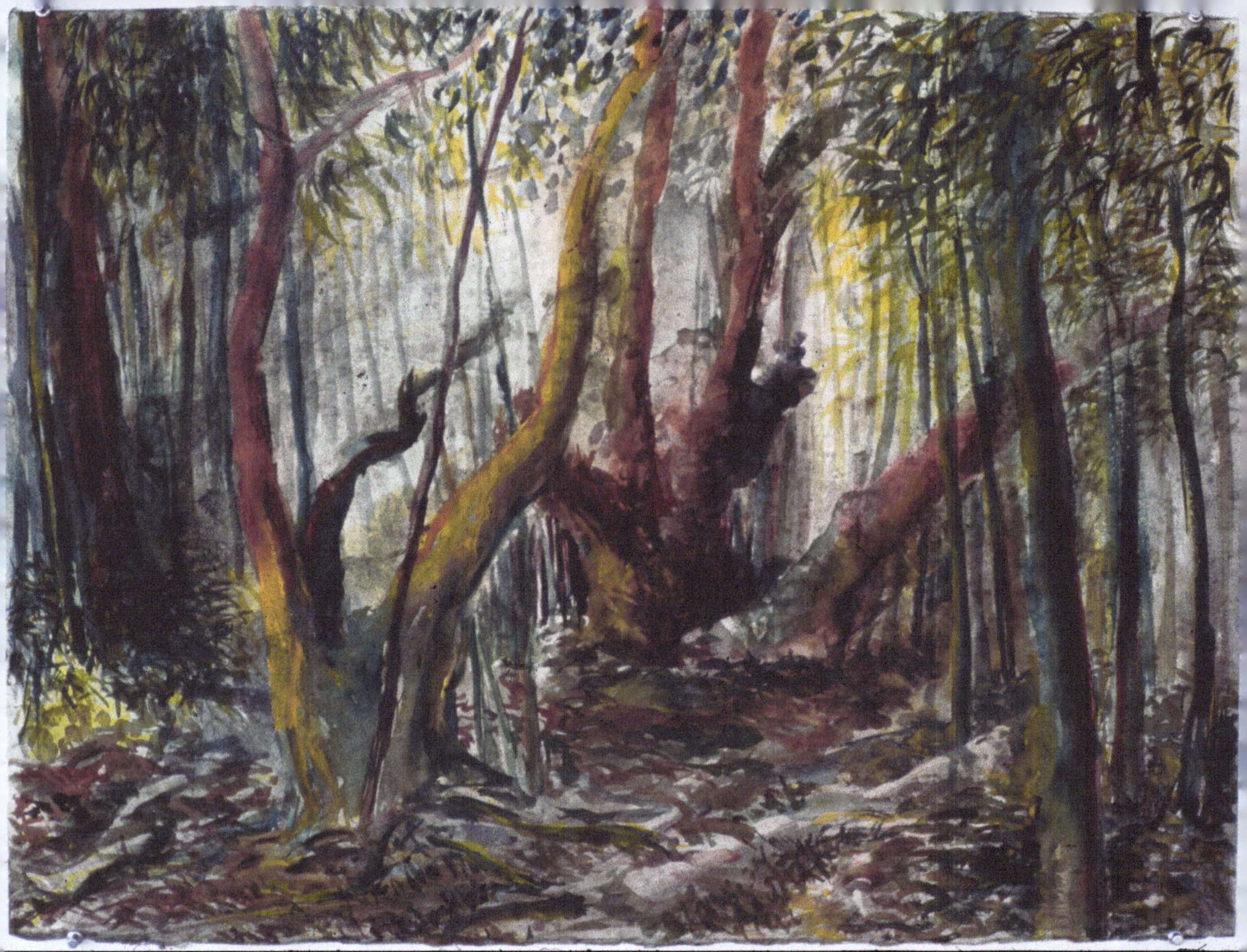

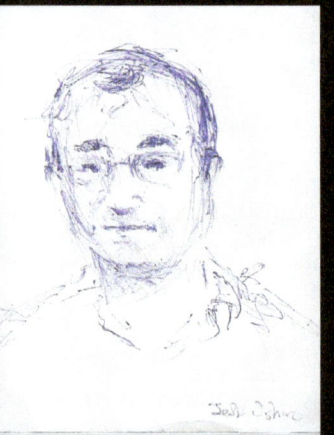

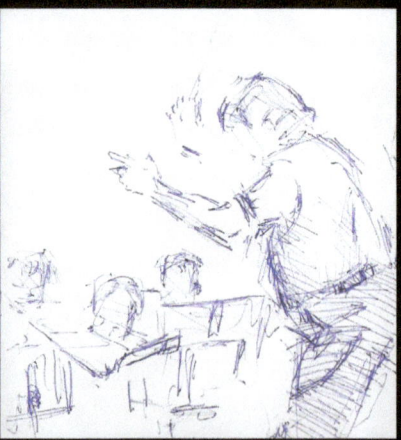

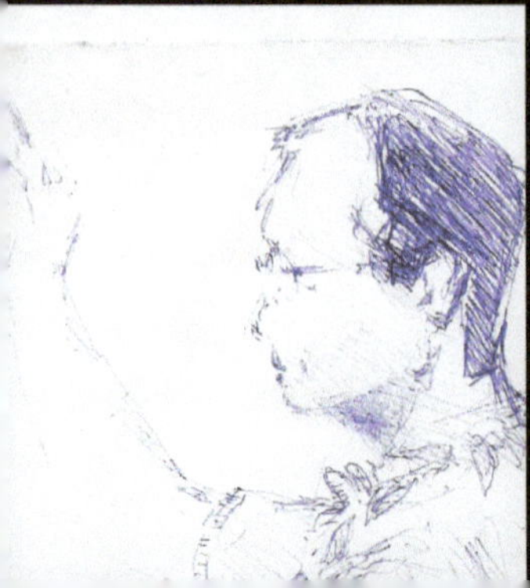

The Torn Red Tree Within the Bamboo Grove,
watercolor

Mr. Oshiro and the Central Middle School Band,
2004, ink sketches

Next Page:

Kikaida Playing Hanafuda for World Domination,
2003, oil on panel

Lenka and Sidemachine, From *Da Blalas: Dad Goes to School*
2015, digital

Lenka, From *Da Blalas: Dad Goes to School*
2015, digital

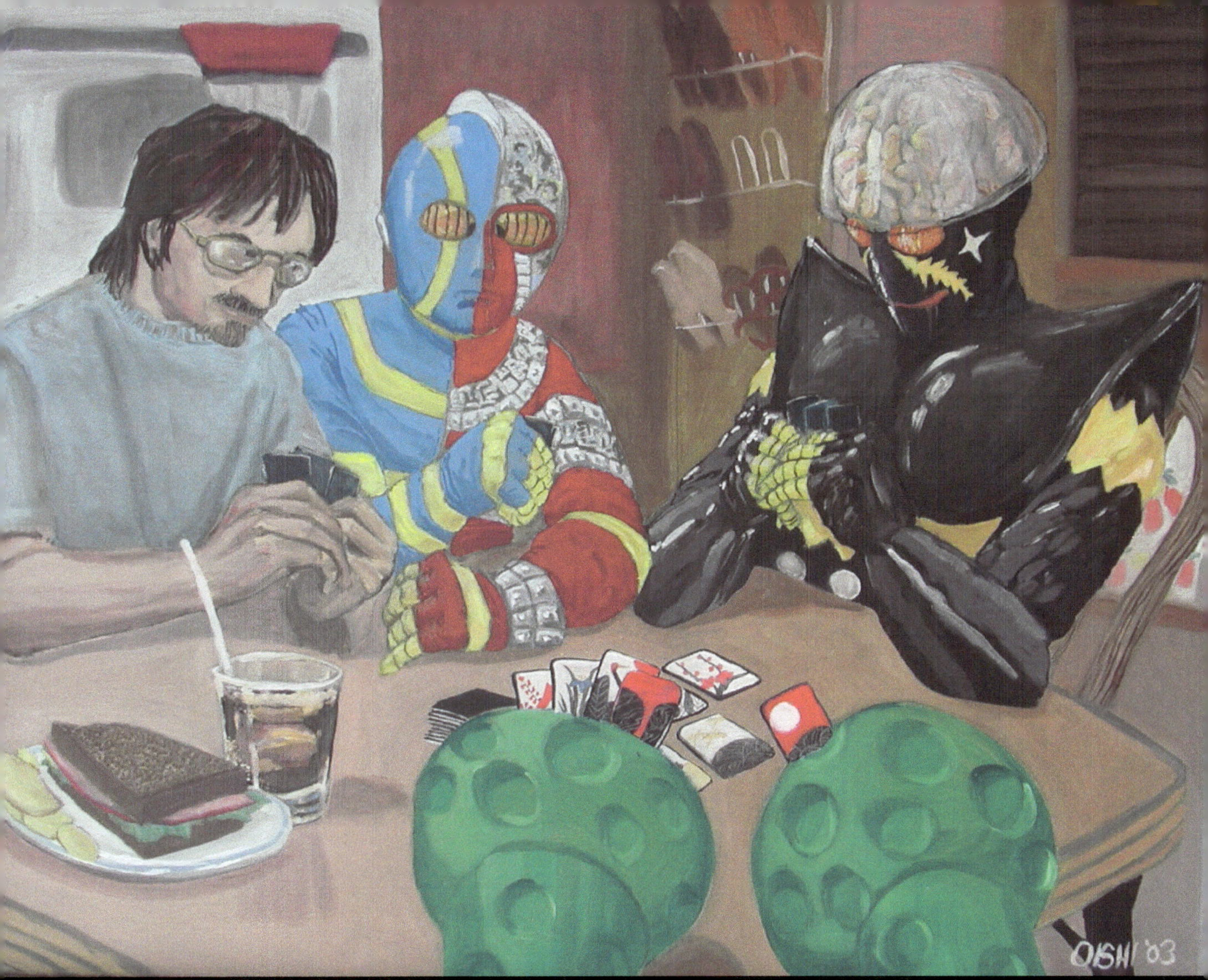

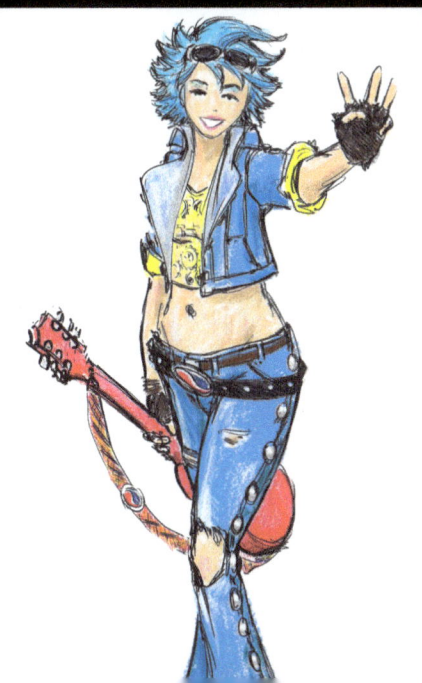

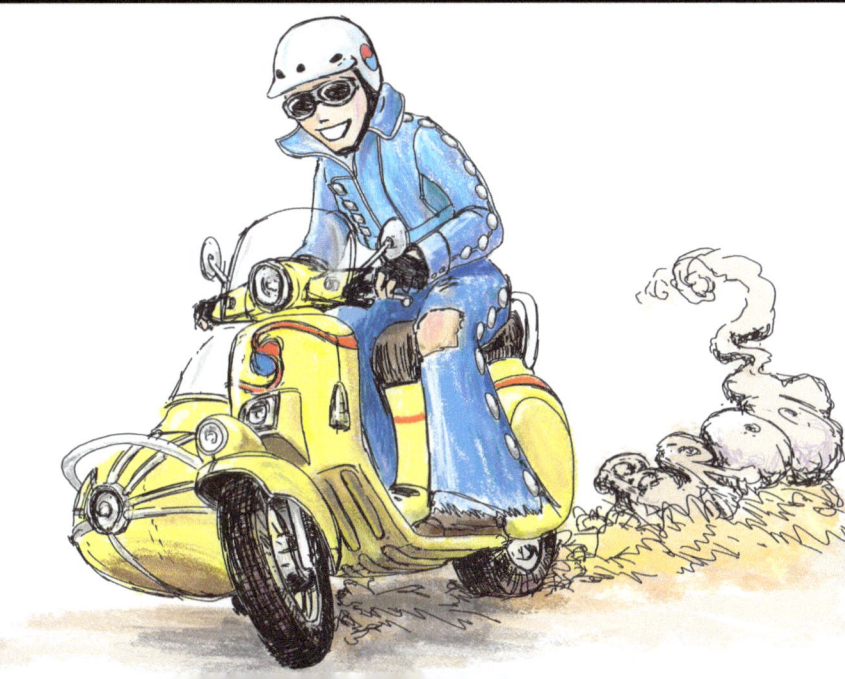

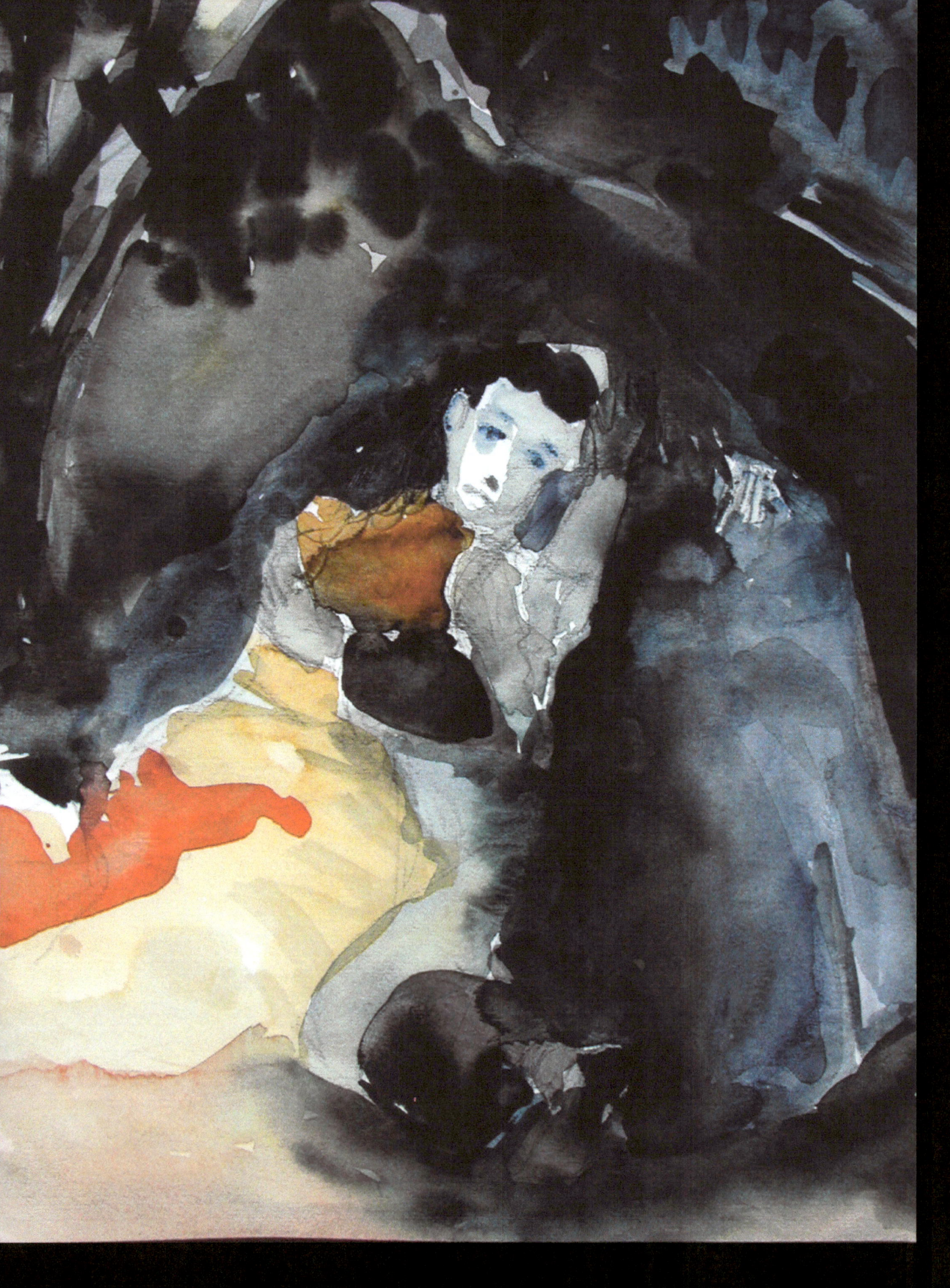

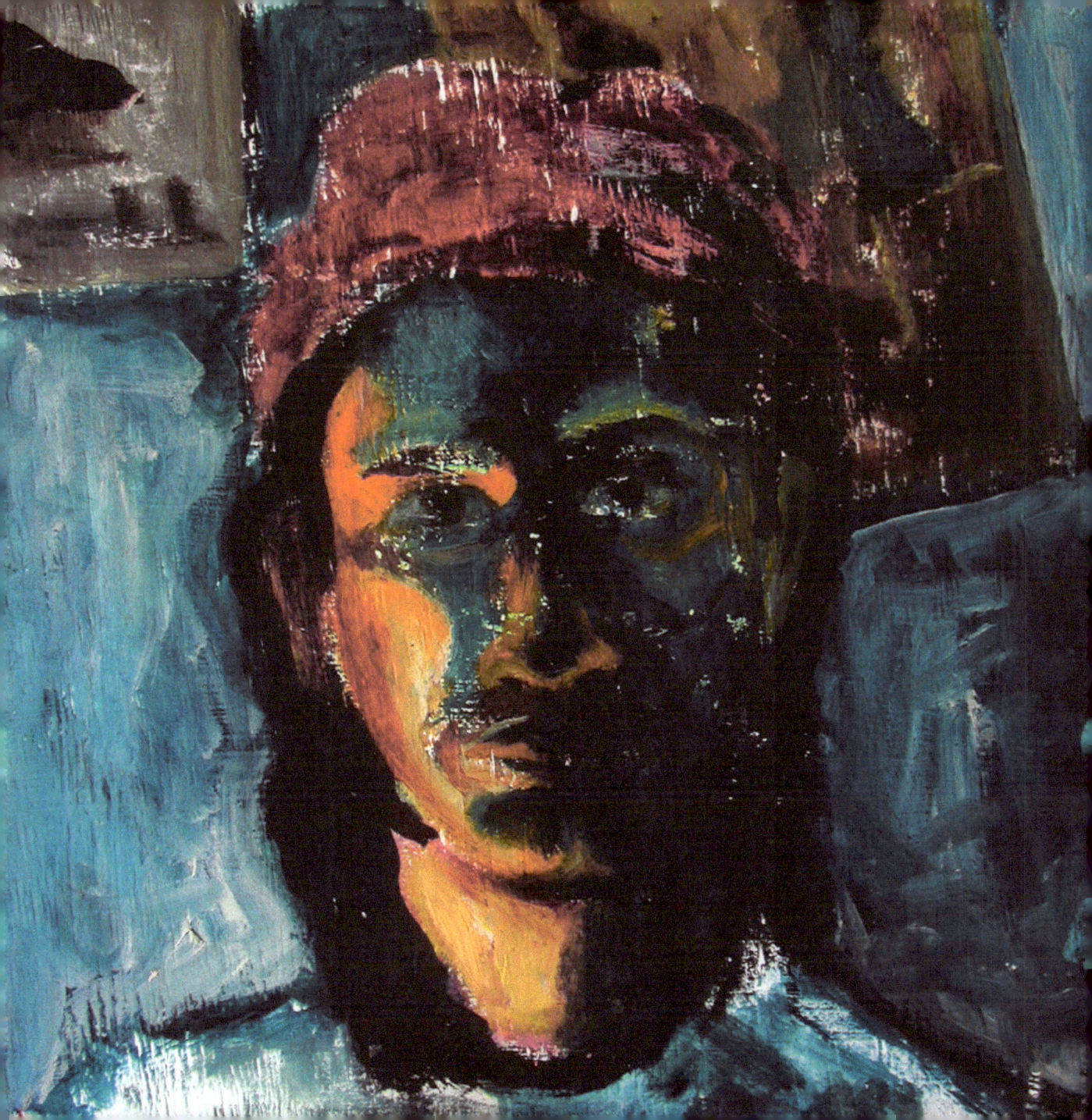

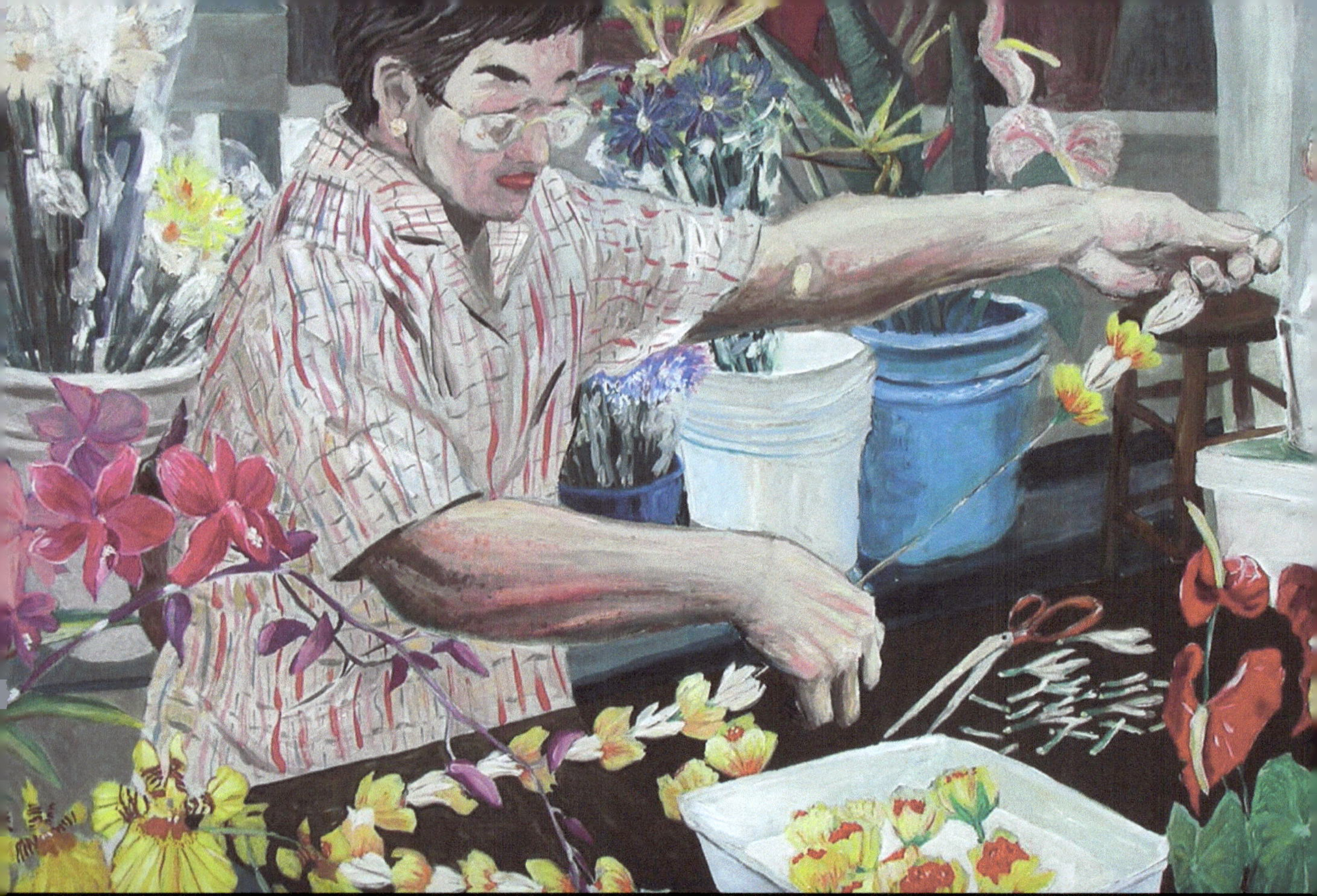

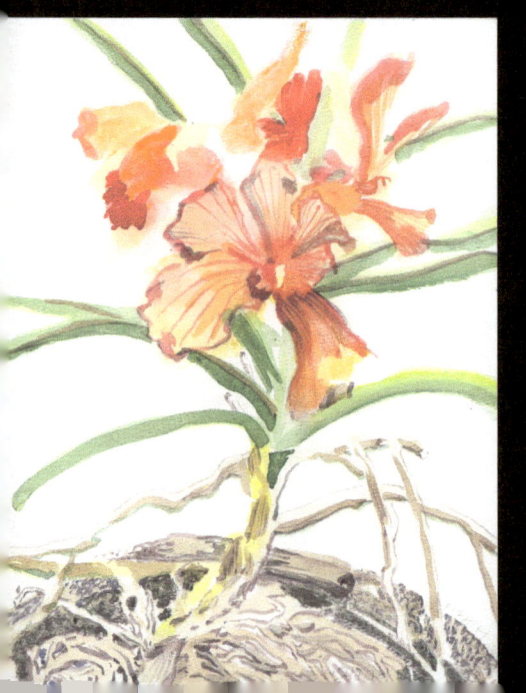

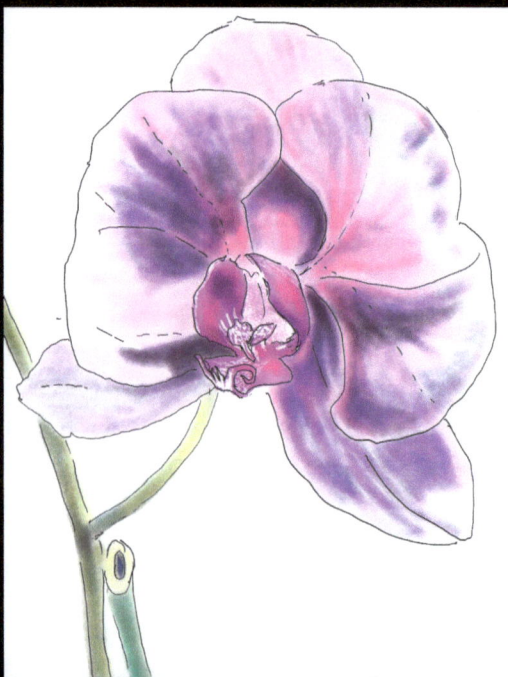

Clockwise from top left:

The Flower Shop, 2002-2003, oil on panel

Orchid, 2013, digital

Orchid, 2014, watercolor

Next Page

Debbie, 1990, sumi ink

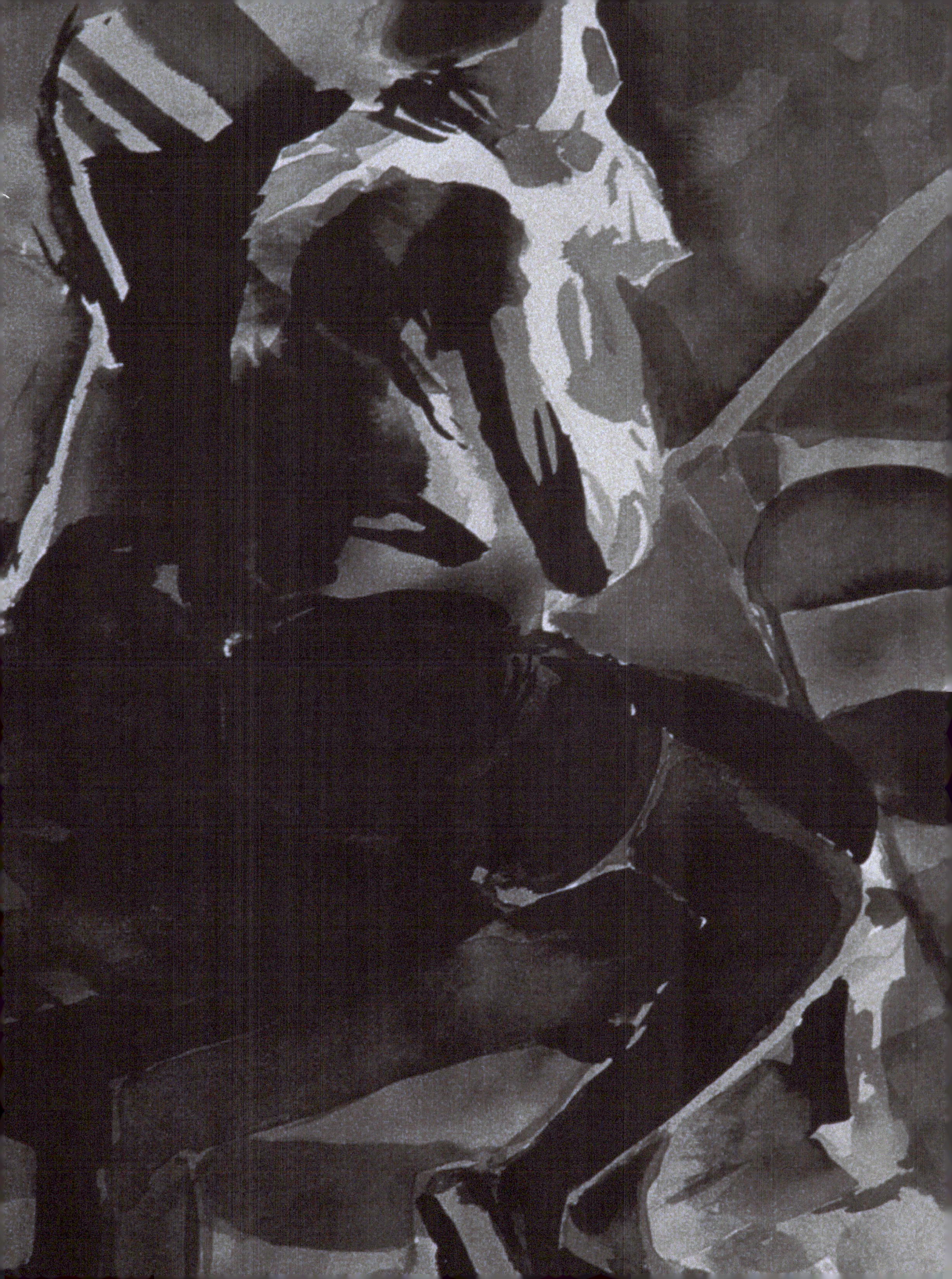

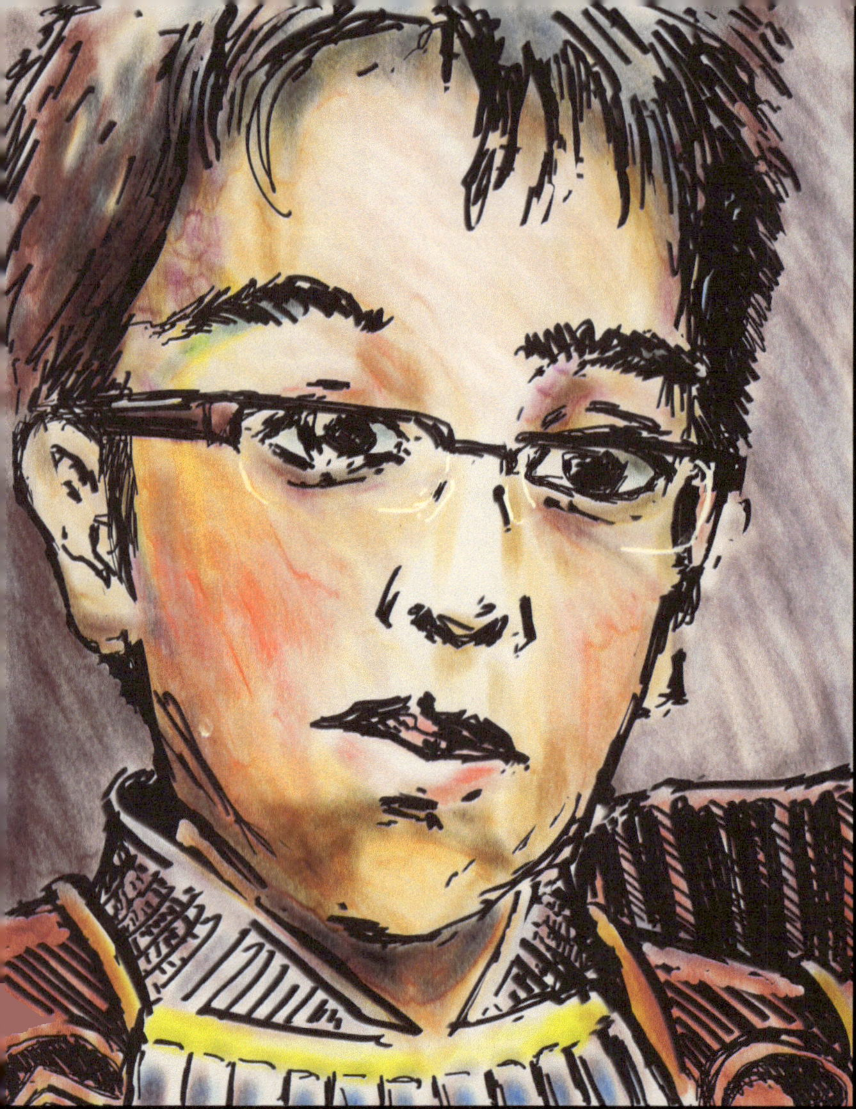

Armor
2016, digital

Kay,
2016, ink

Figure Drawing,
watercolor

Next page:

*Kay Drawing at Koganji
Temple,* Poster Version for:
MangaBento Exhibit: Maiden
Craft
2016, digital, ink

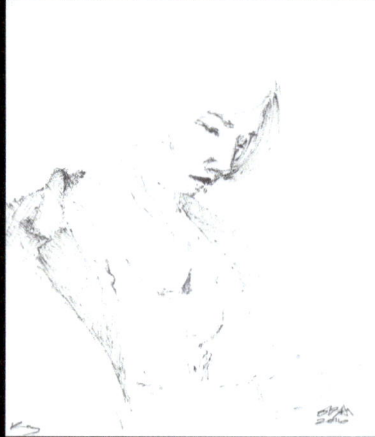

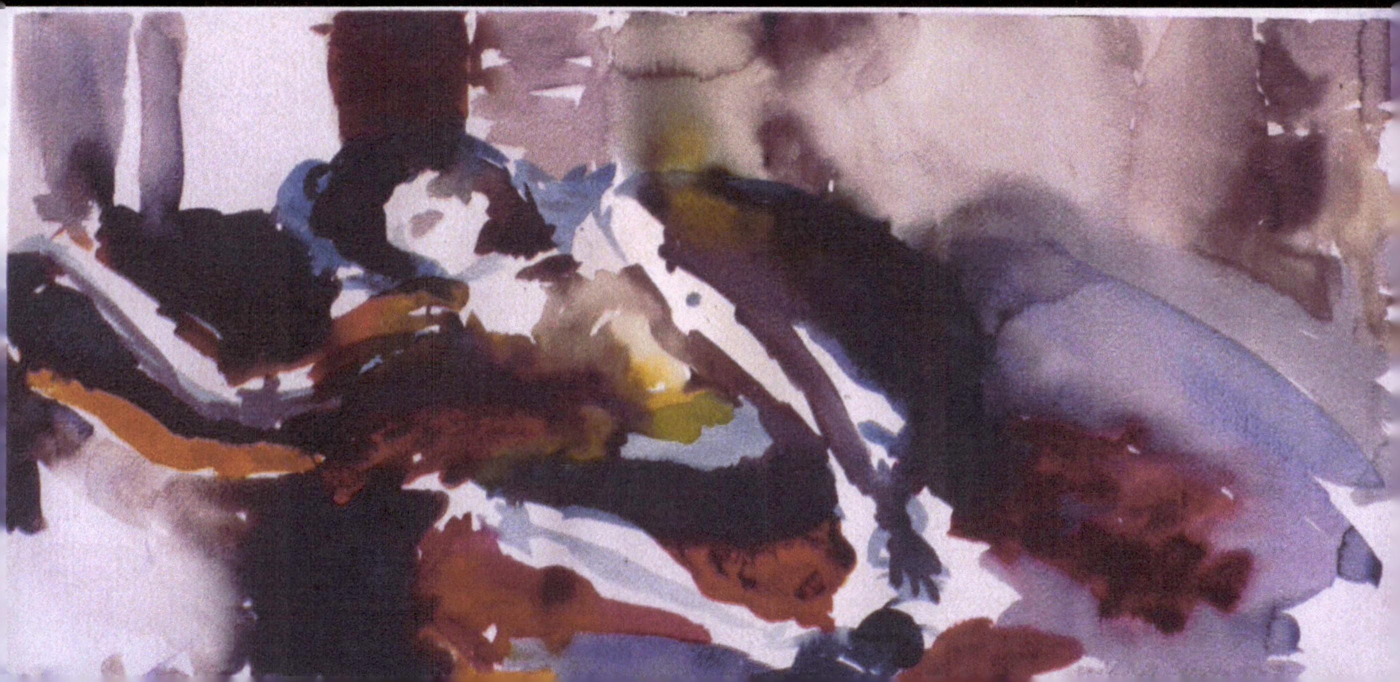

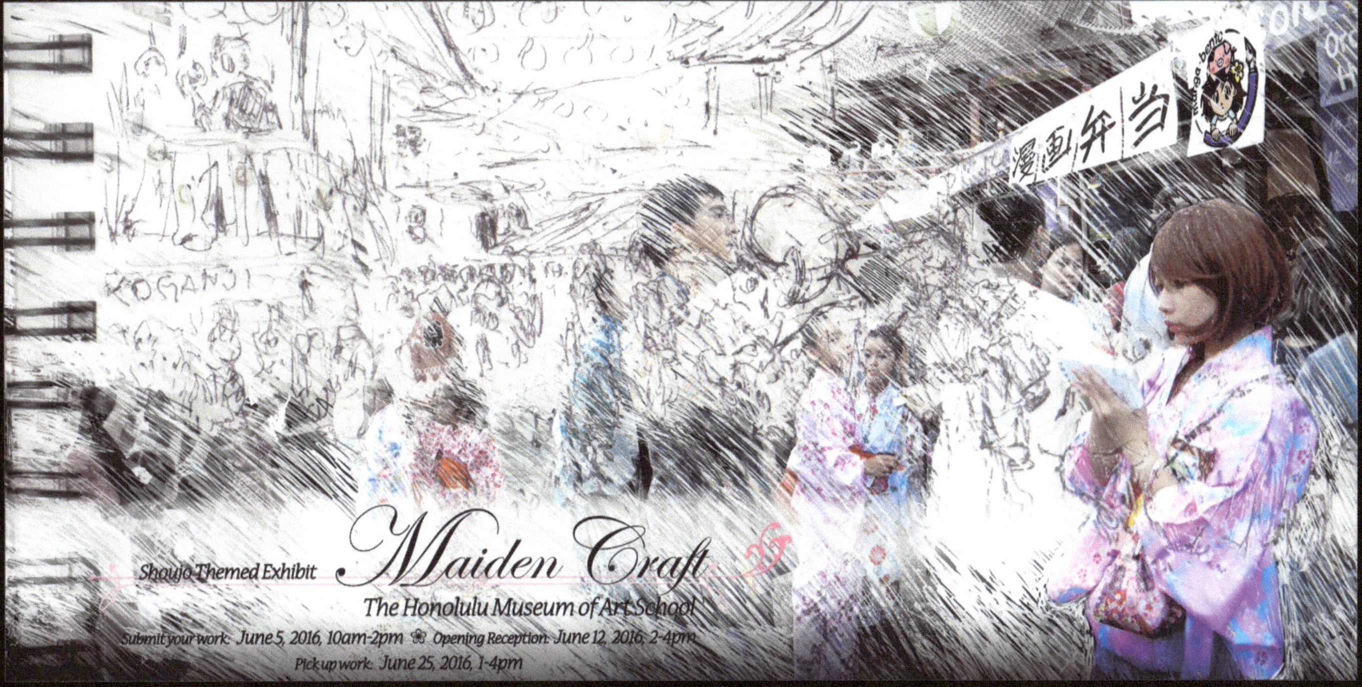

Shoujo Themed Exhibit *Maiden Craft*

The Honolulu Museum of Art School

Submit your work: June 5, 2016, 10am-2pm ❀ Opening Reception: June 12, 2016, 2-4pm

Pick up work: June 25, 2016, 1-4pm

The Bridge Between Worlds,
2016, digital, model KissingDolls

Ānuenue, the rainbow bridge between worlds was fading. Usagi Shiro, Lapakikea as her neighbors called her, did not want to step into the mirky waters of the present which undoubtably led to an uncertain future. She wanted desperately to stay in the past she knew and loved yet did not want to fade away nor be left behind as the past must be. Her friends had gone forward, cheering her on as they pushed past her. The ripples of their passage were fading. But it was so much easier too stay as she was. . .

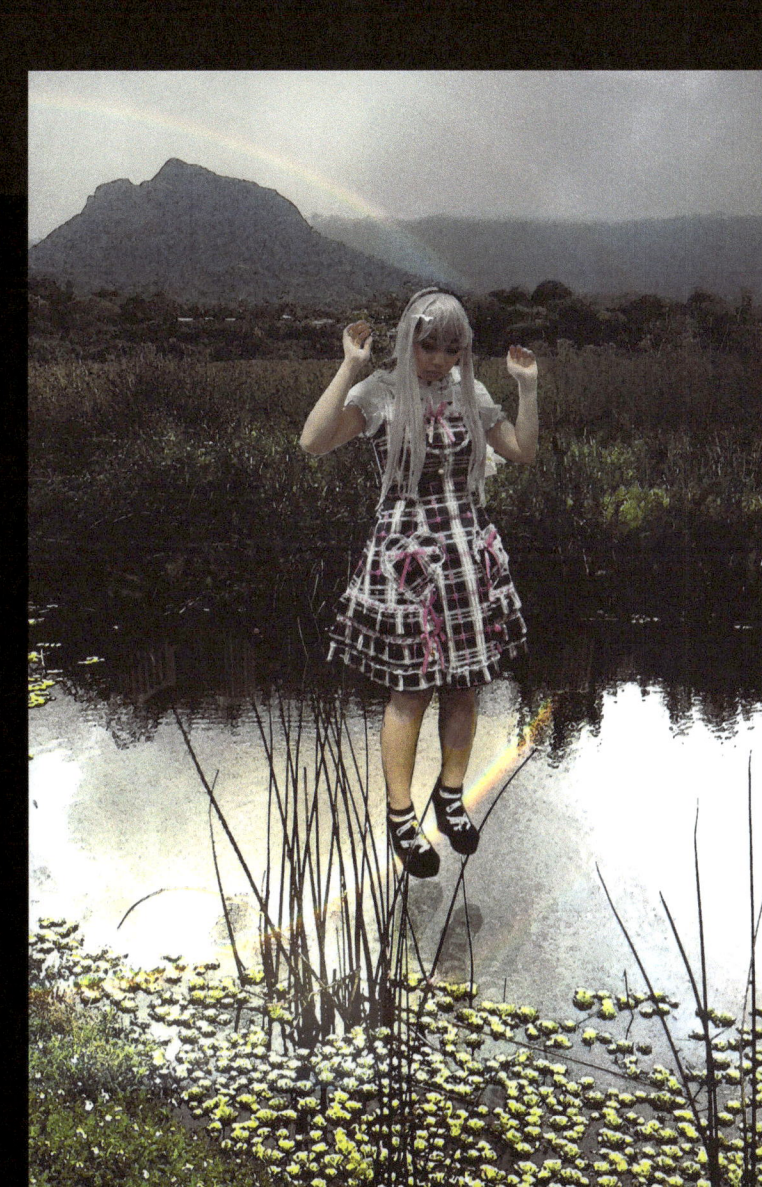

. . . time. to continue into the future riding the river of and she missed them dearly. But it was easier Many of her friends had stayed in the past things were good, but much had gone awry. a better future by returning to the past? Some away from the future. Perhaps she could build be no problem to leave the present and turn that she loved. While the bridge held it would neighbors called her, looked back into the past was fading. Usagi Shiro, Lapakikea as her Ānuenue, the rainbow bridge between worlds

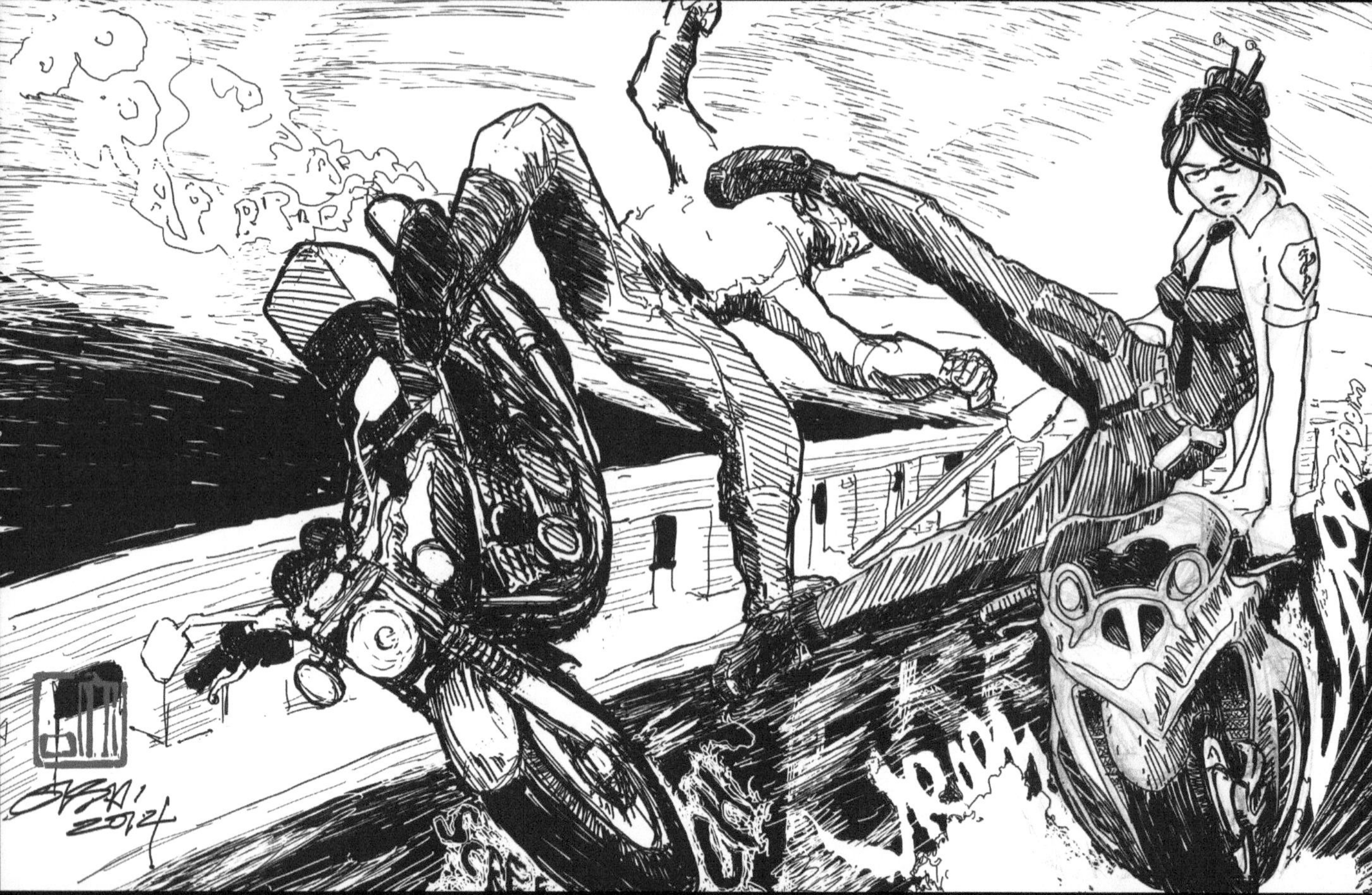

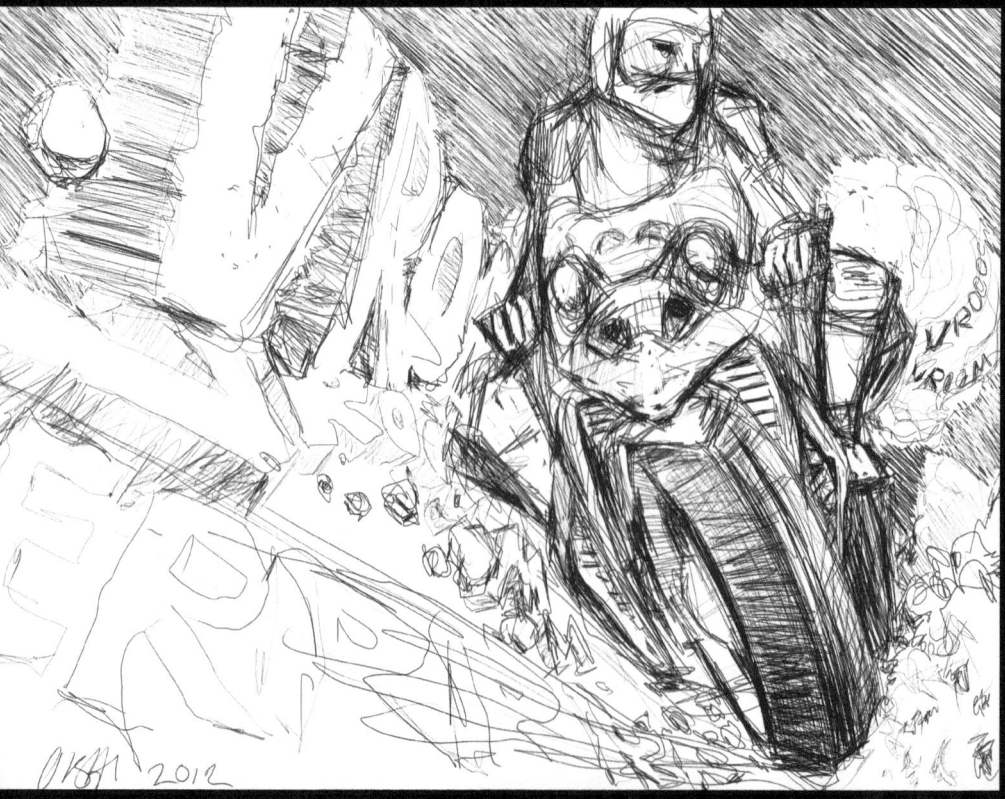

Kira Double Kick,
Cover Art for *Grass-cutter Kusanagi*
2014, digital

Vrrroom!
2012, digital

Next page:

Suminator,
2012, digital

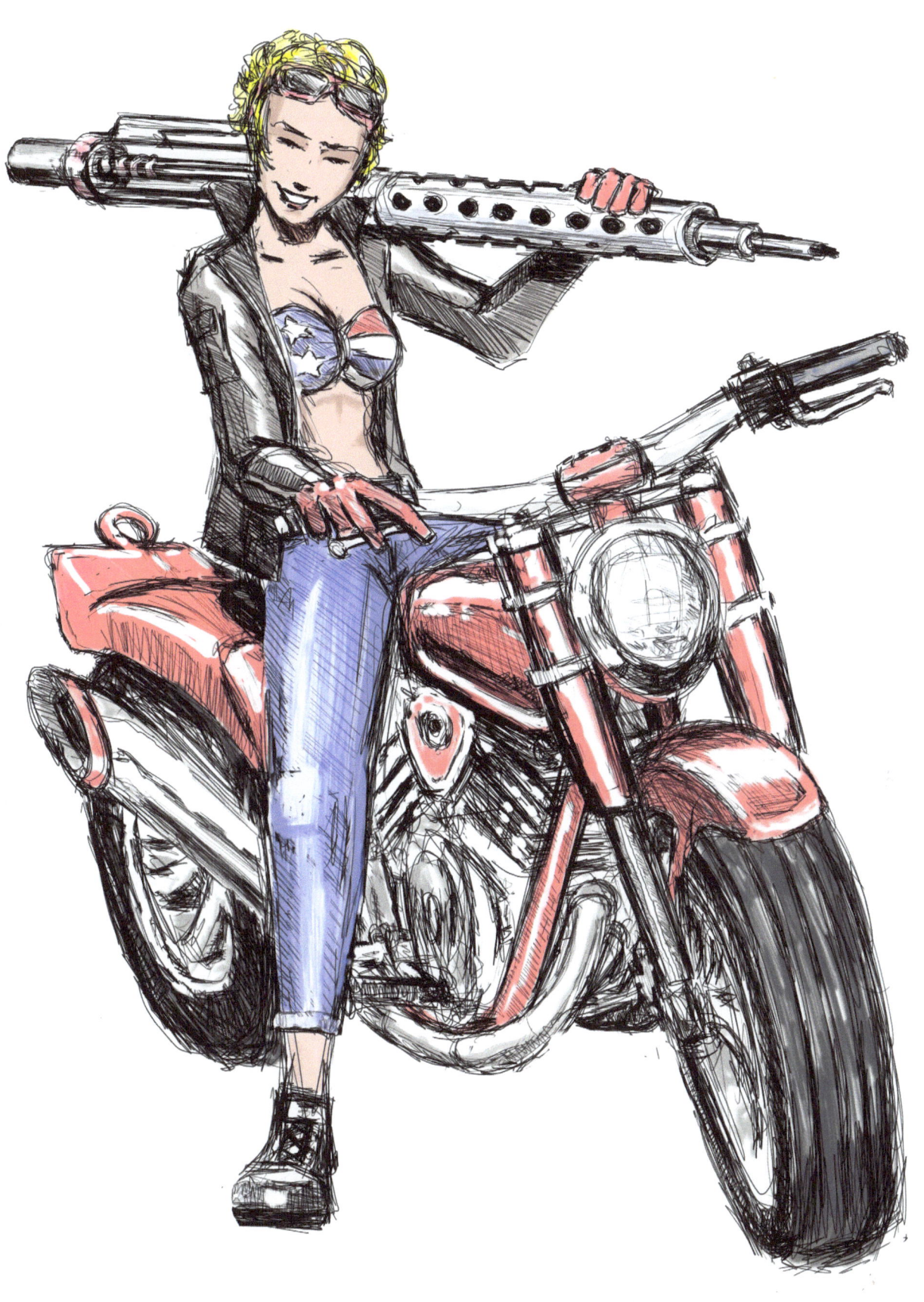

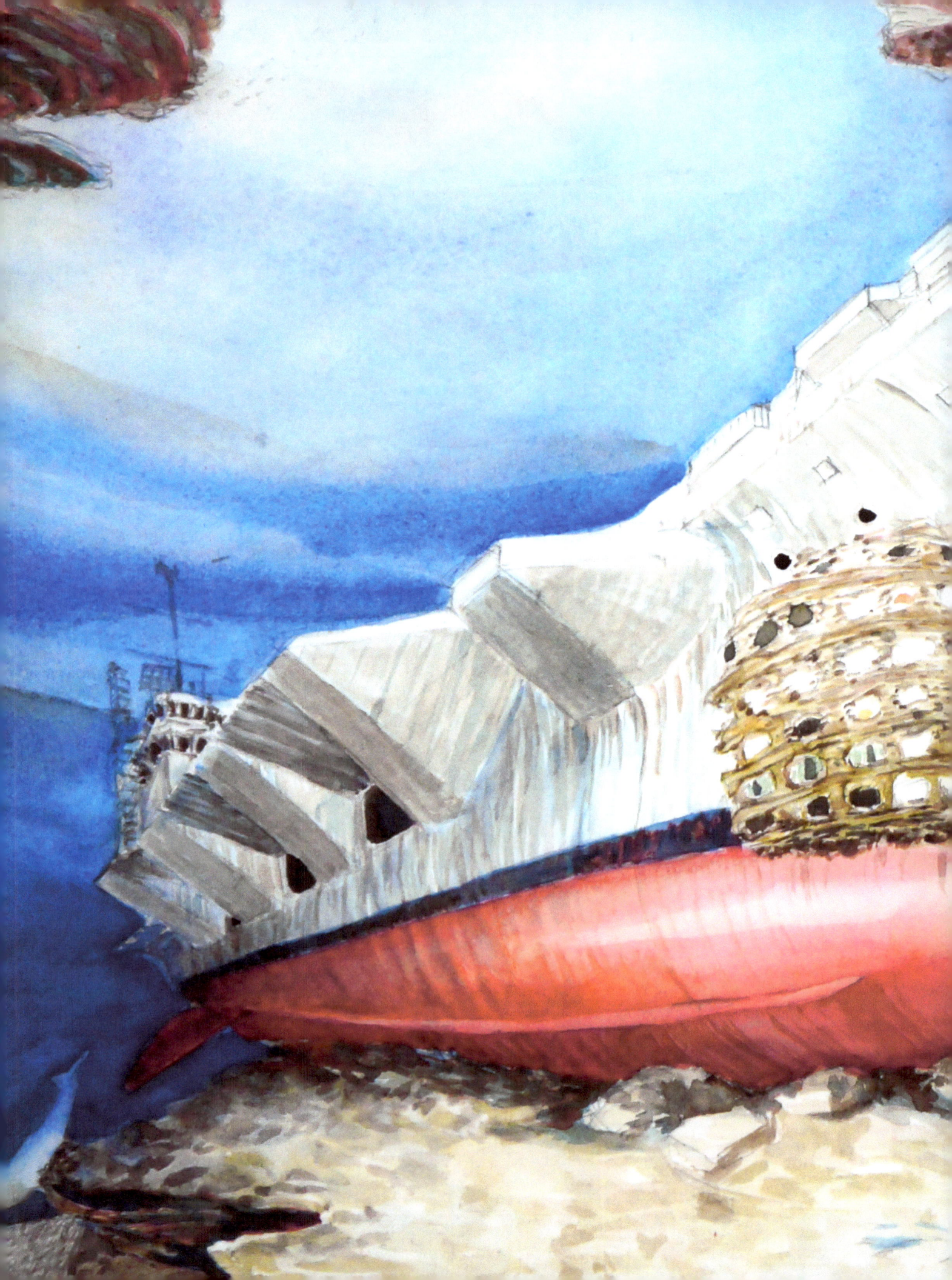

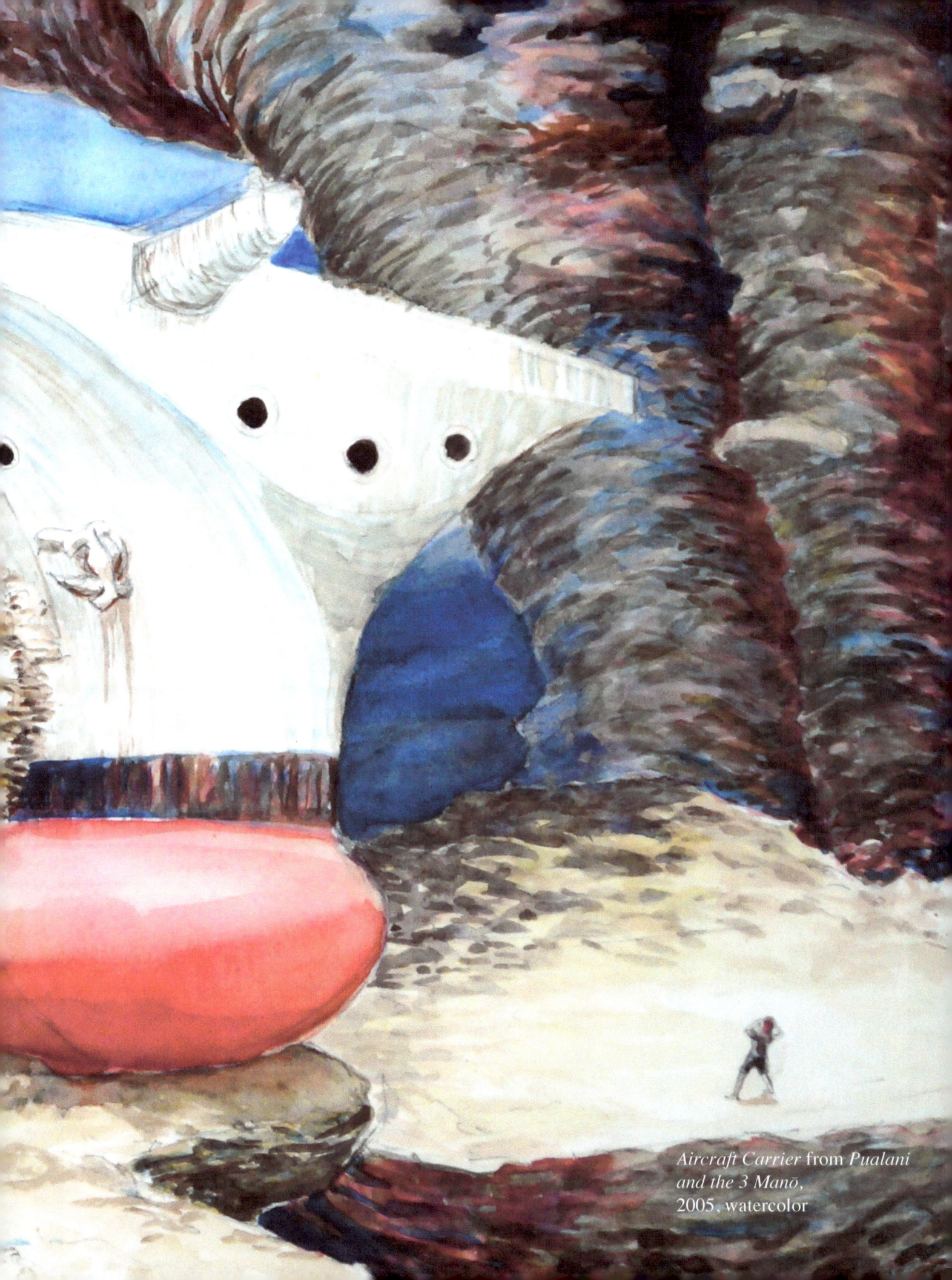

Aircraft Carrier from *Pualani
and the 3 Manō*,
2005, watercolor

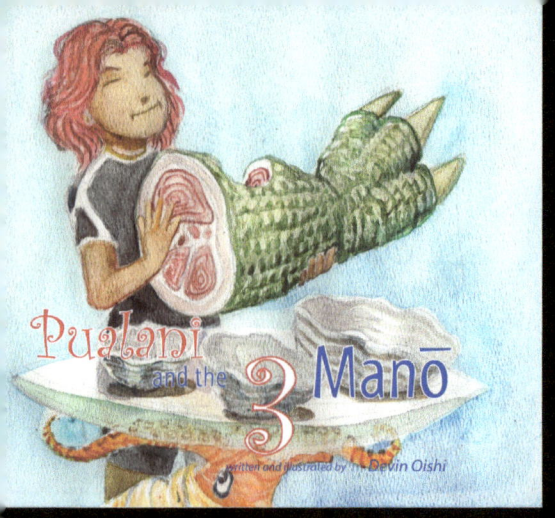

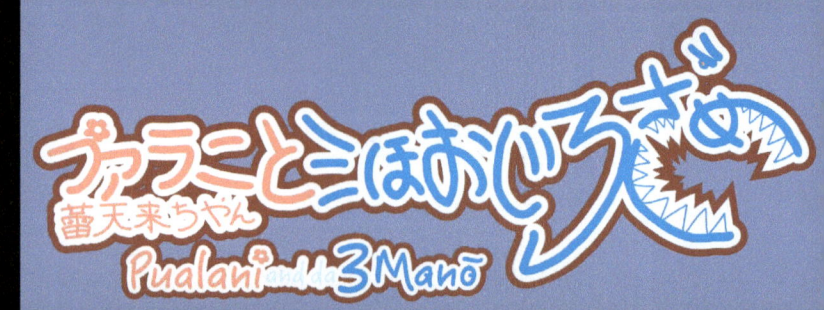

Pualani and the 3 Manō, 2nd Edition
Cover Art
2015, digital and watercolor

Pualani and the 3 Manō,
Logo Graffic Japanese Edition
2016, digital

Da Blala's in the Manō's Hale Cover Art
2014, digital and watercolor

She's in My Chair! Interior Illustration
from *Pualani and the 3 Manō*
watercolor

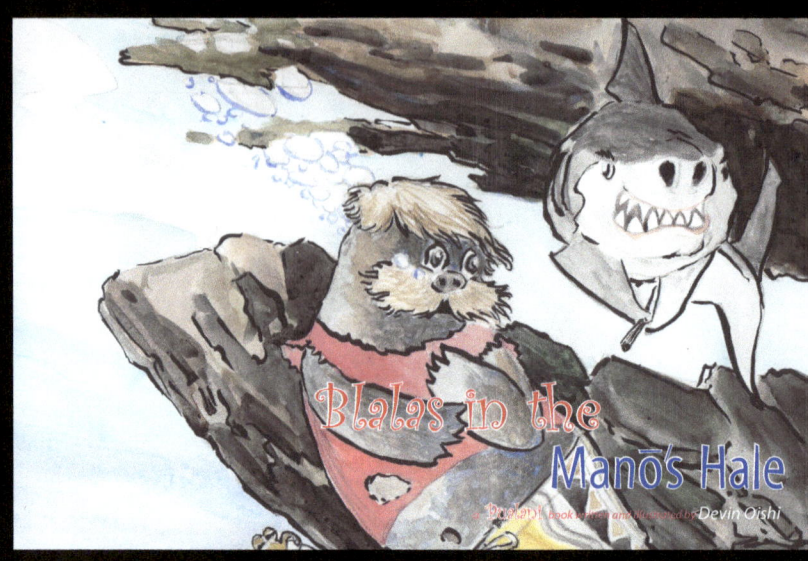

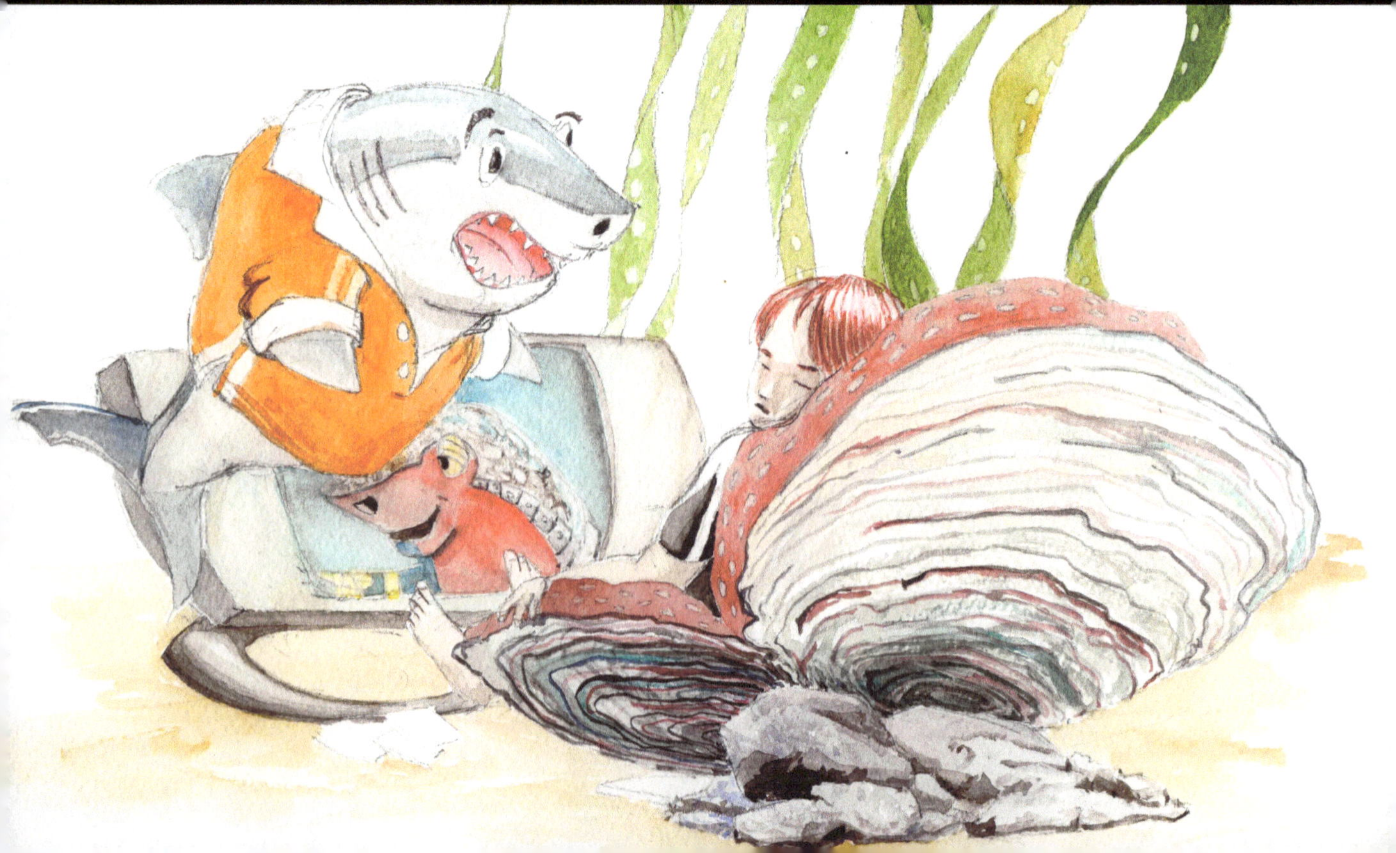

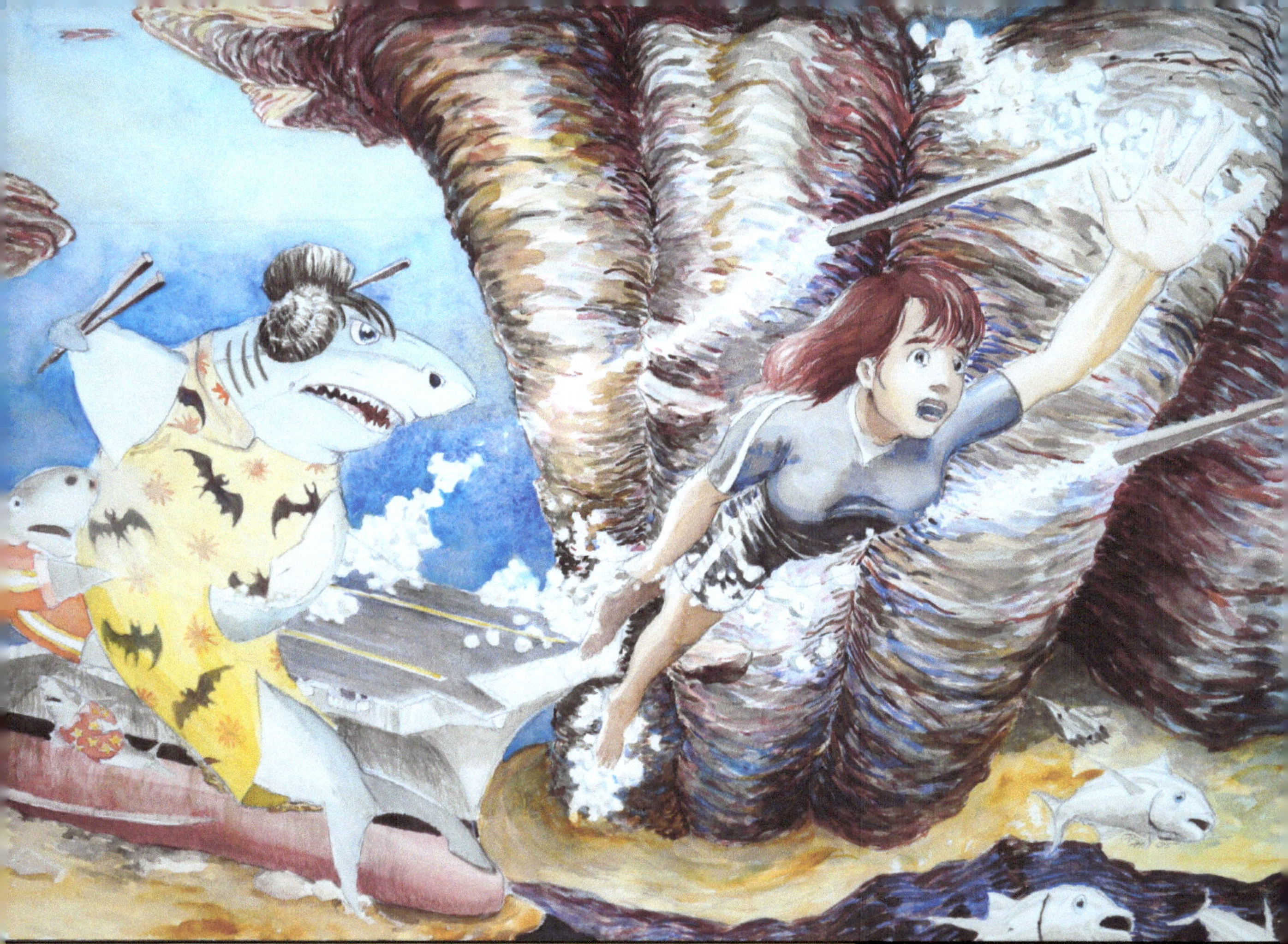

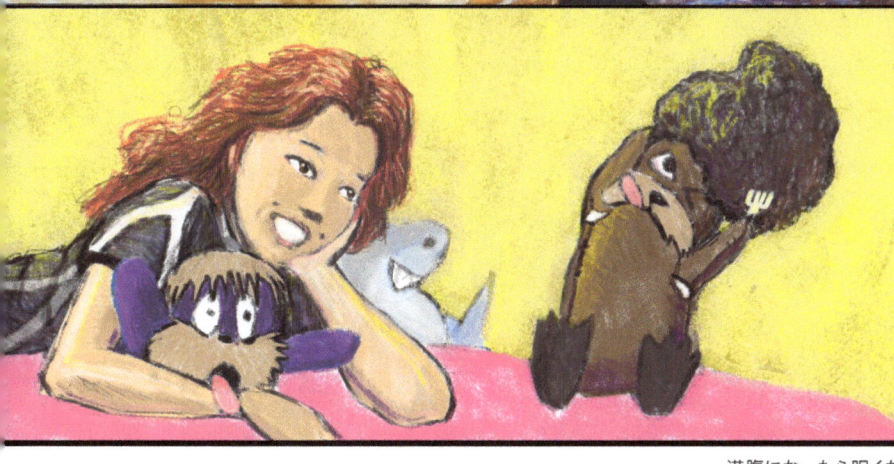

満腹になったら眠くなった。プアはチョット休もうとした。「ウワー、この椅子は超柔らかい!」

Sleepy after her enormous meal, Pua looked for a place to rest. "Ho dis chair too soft!"

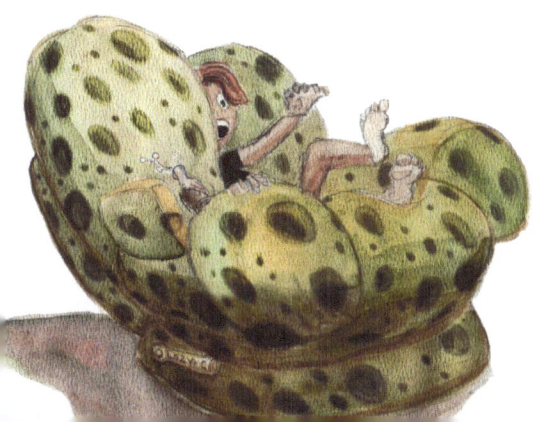

Pualani and the 3 Manō, Interior Illustration 2005, watercolor

Da Blala's in the Manō's Hale Interior Illustration 2014, digital

Dis Chair Too Soft! Interior Layout, *Pualani and the 3 Manō*, 2014, watercolor, graphite, digital

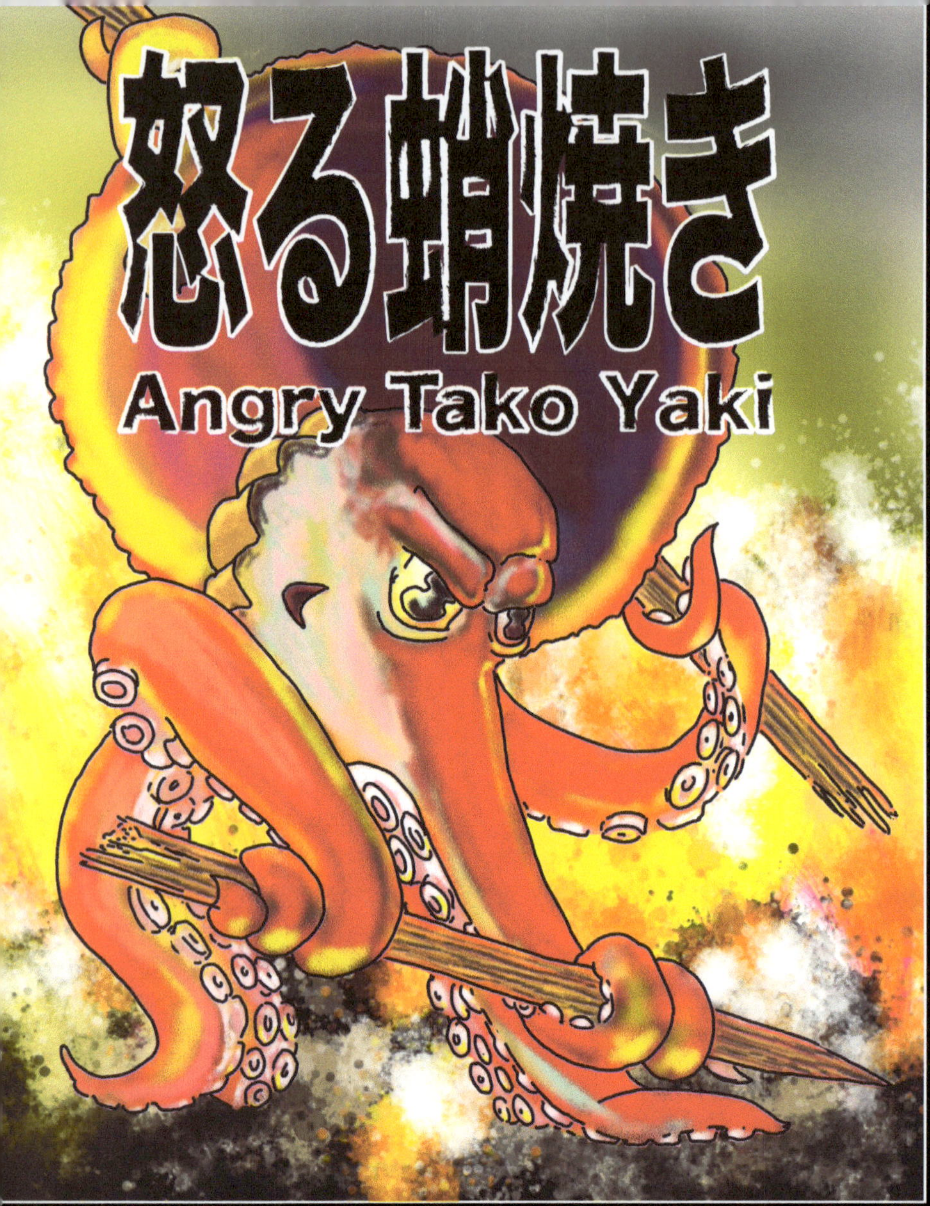

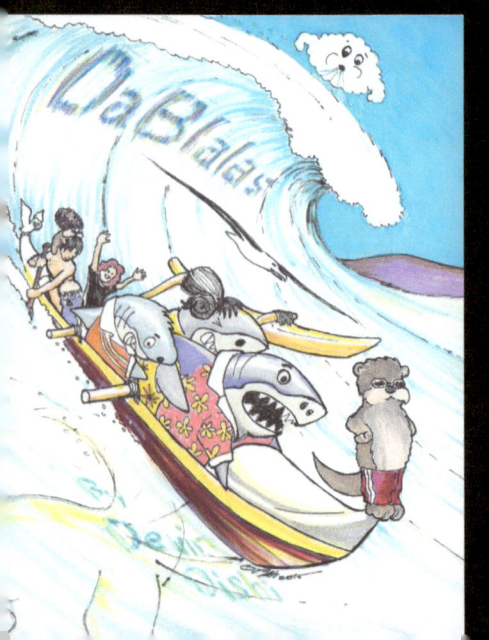

怒る蛸焼き
Angry Tako Yaki

Clockwise:

Cover from short manga, *Angry Takoyaki*,
2012, digital

Cover art from *The Aircraft Carrier Abraham Lincoln*,
2008, digital

Cover art from *Ronin*,
2016, digital

Cover art from *Da Blalas*,
2014, ink

Next page:

47,
2013, digital
One page comic

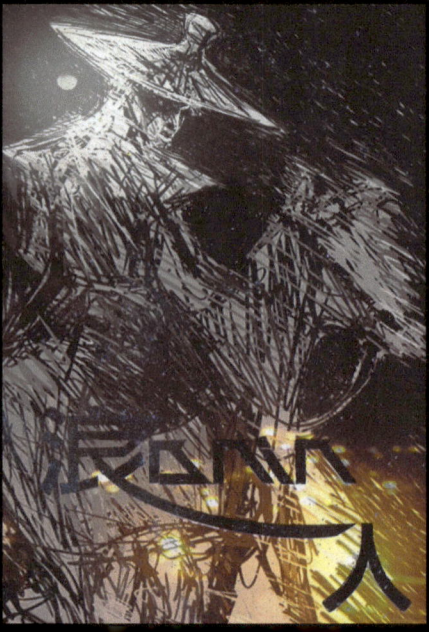

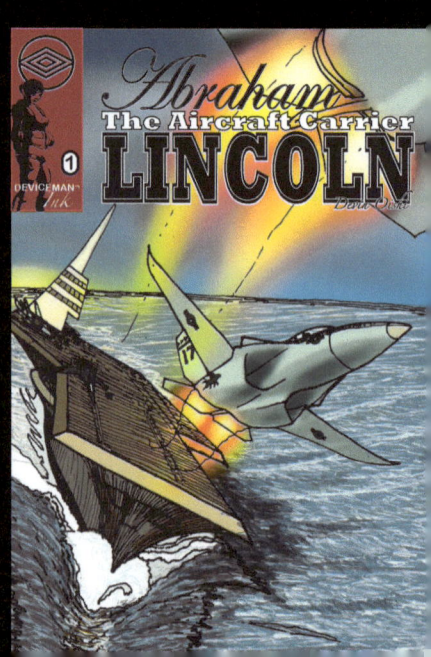

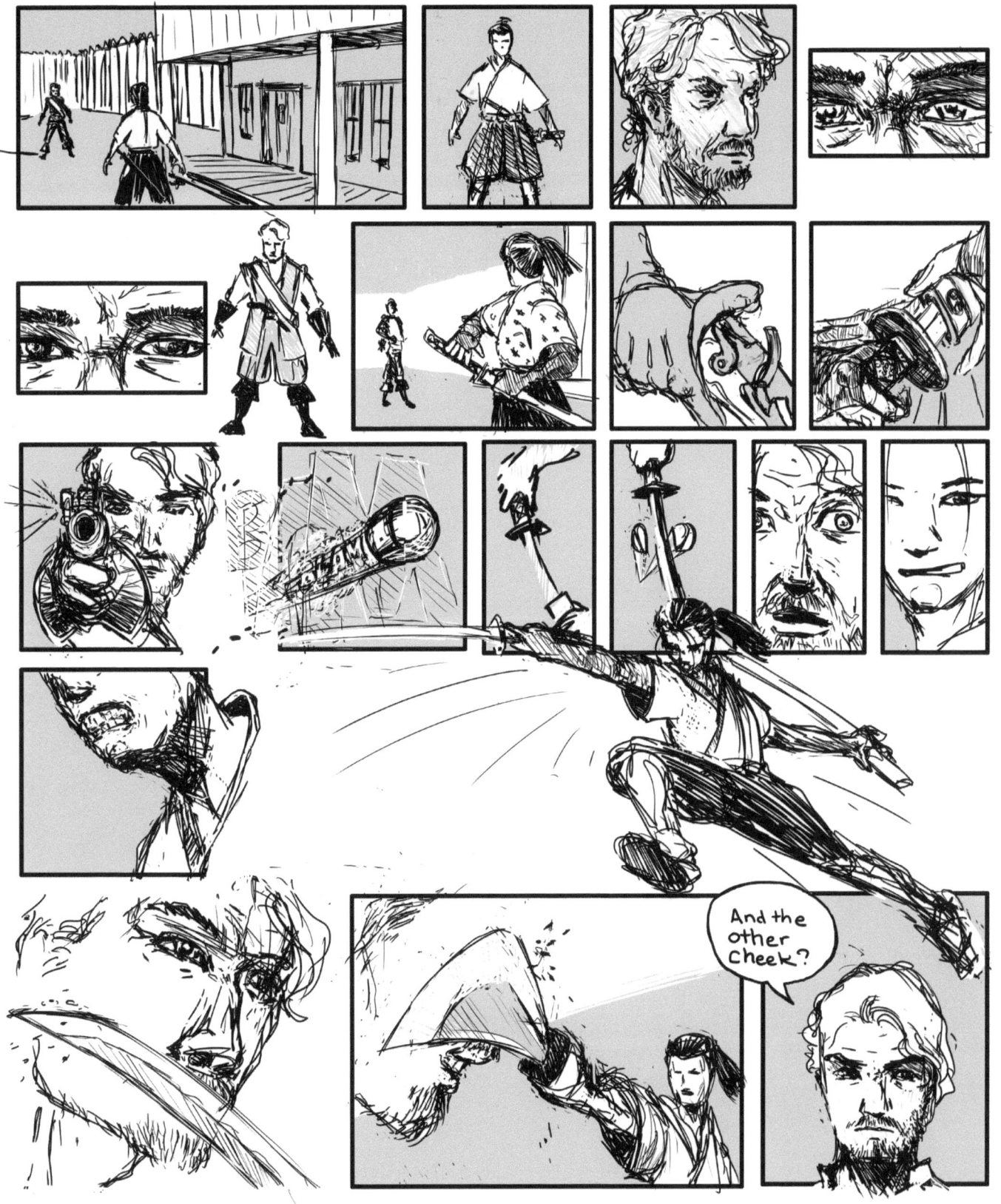

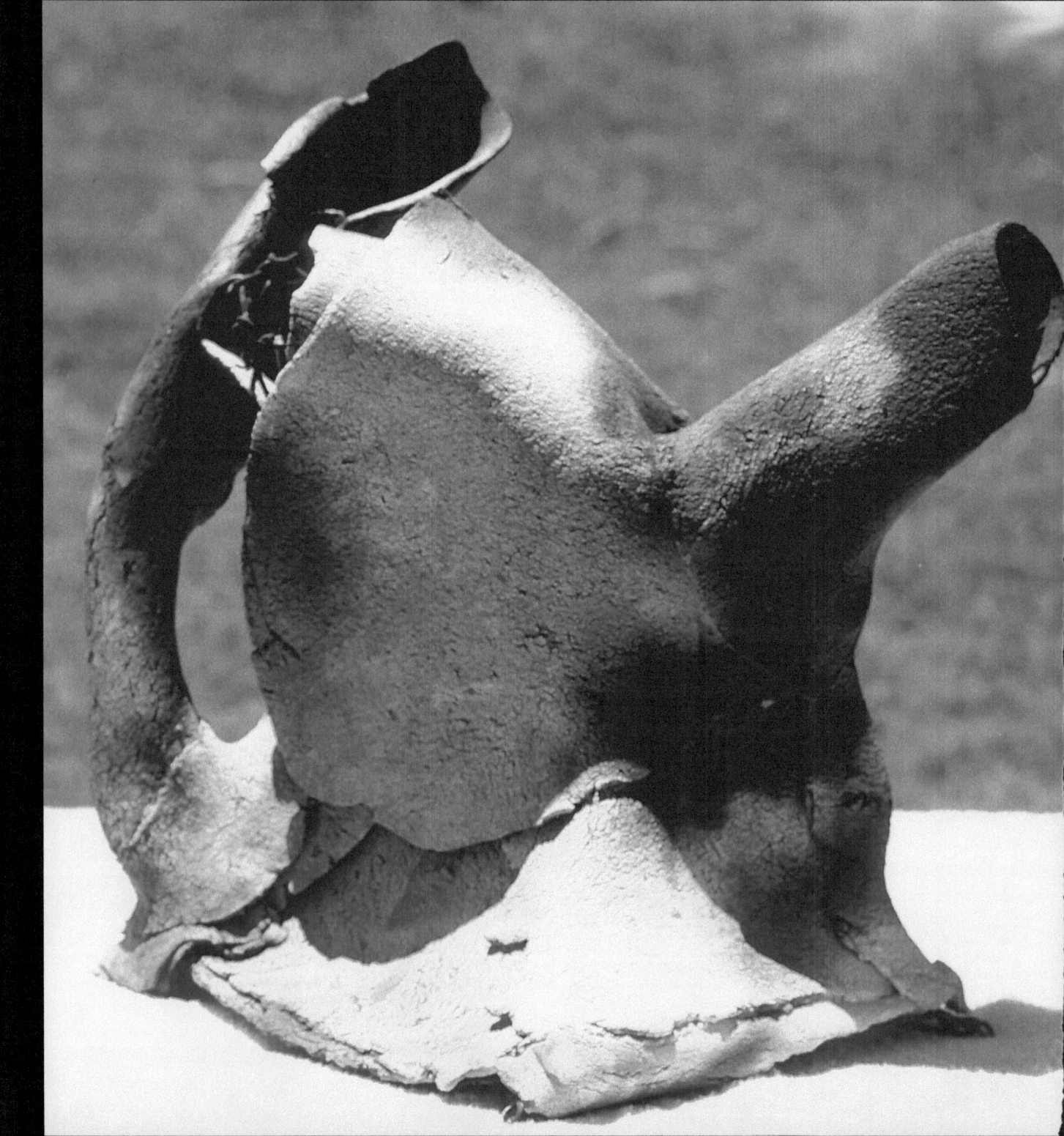

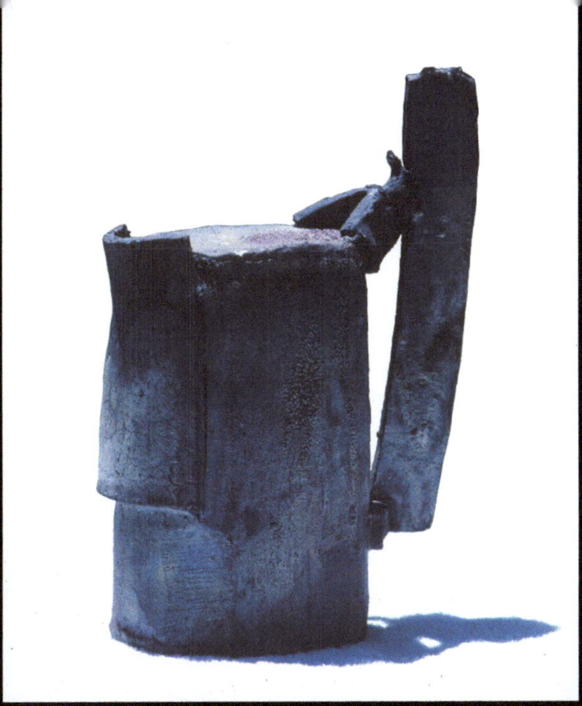

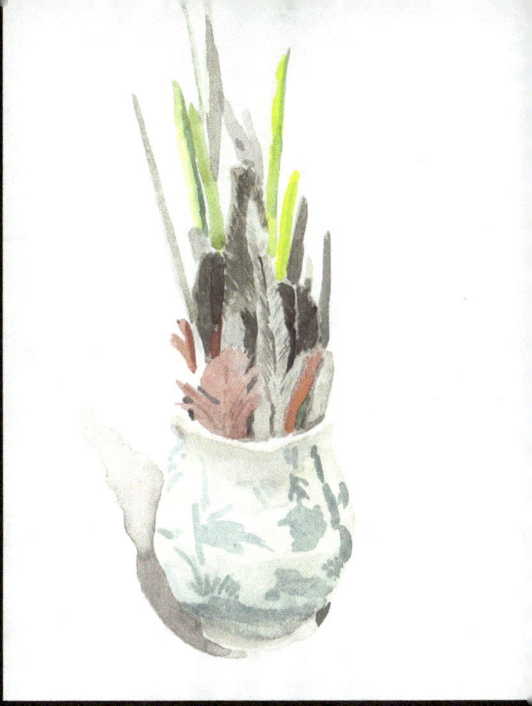

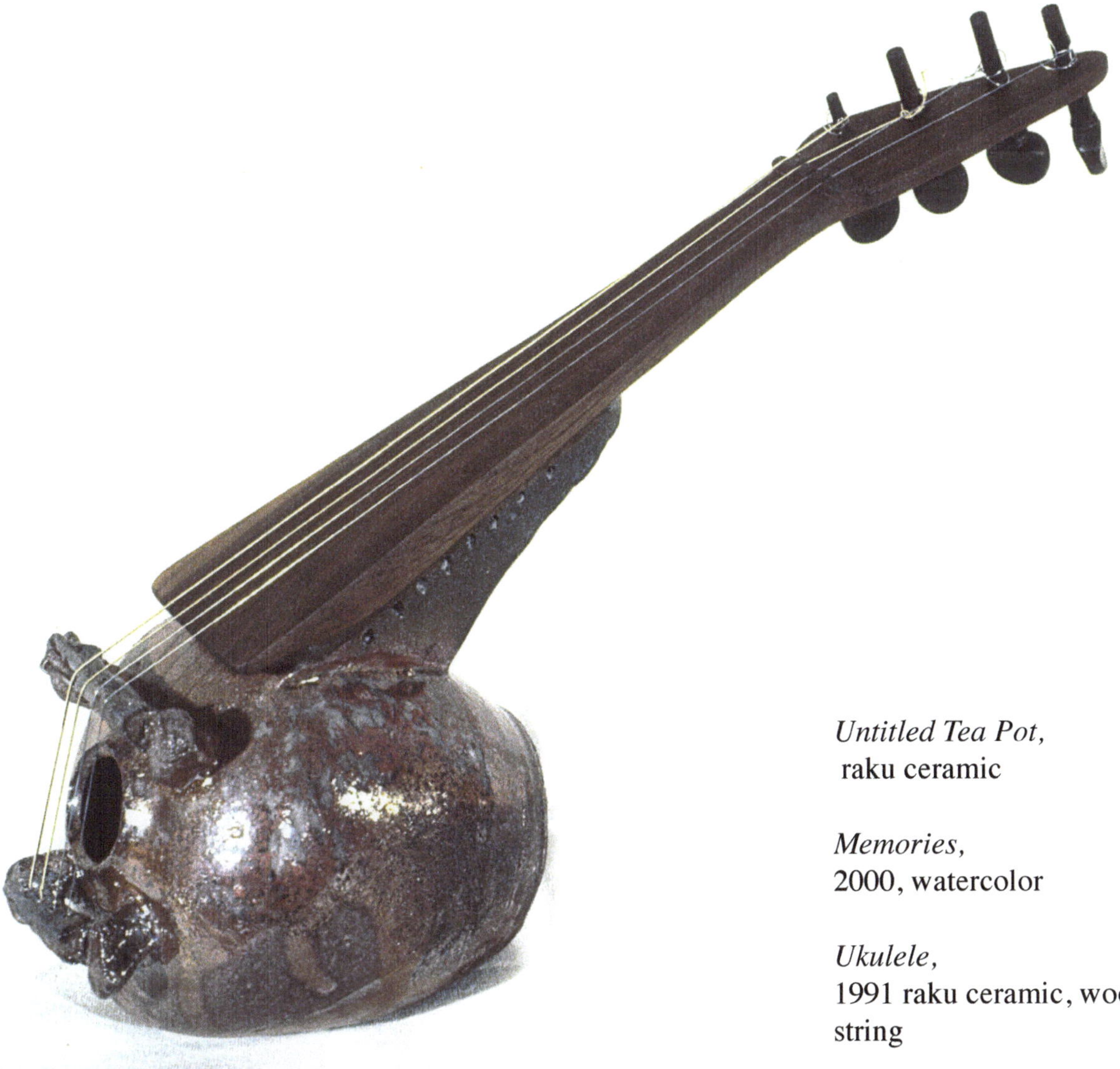

Untitled Tea Pot,
 raku ceramic

Memories,
2000, watercolor

Ukulele,
1991 raku ceramic, wood,
string

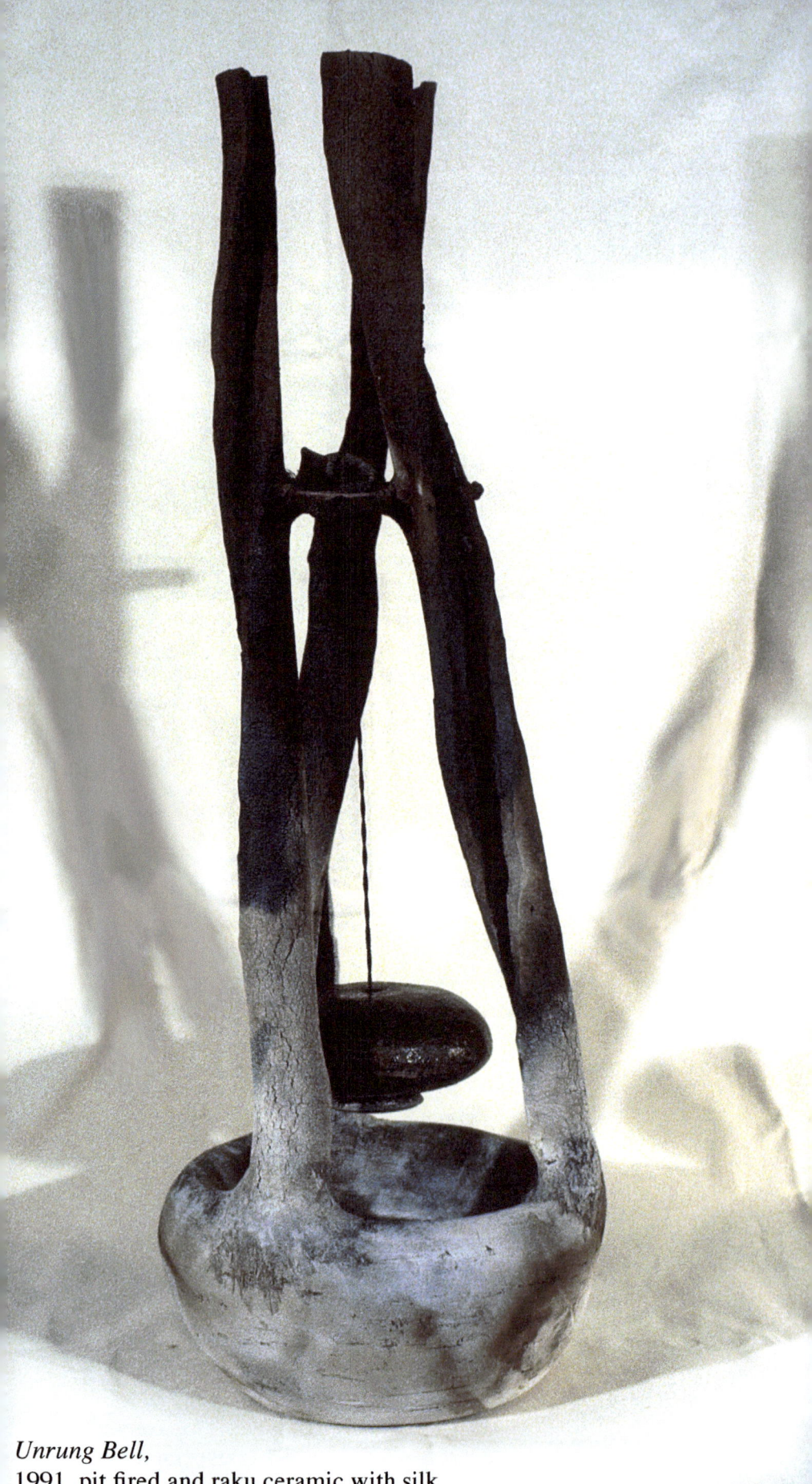

Unrung Bell,
1991, pit fired and raku ceramic with silk

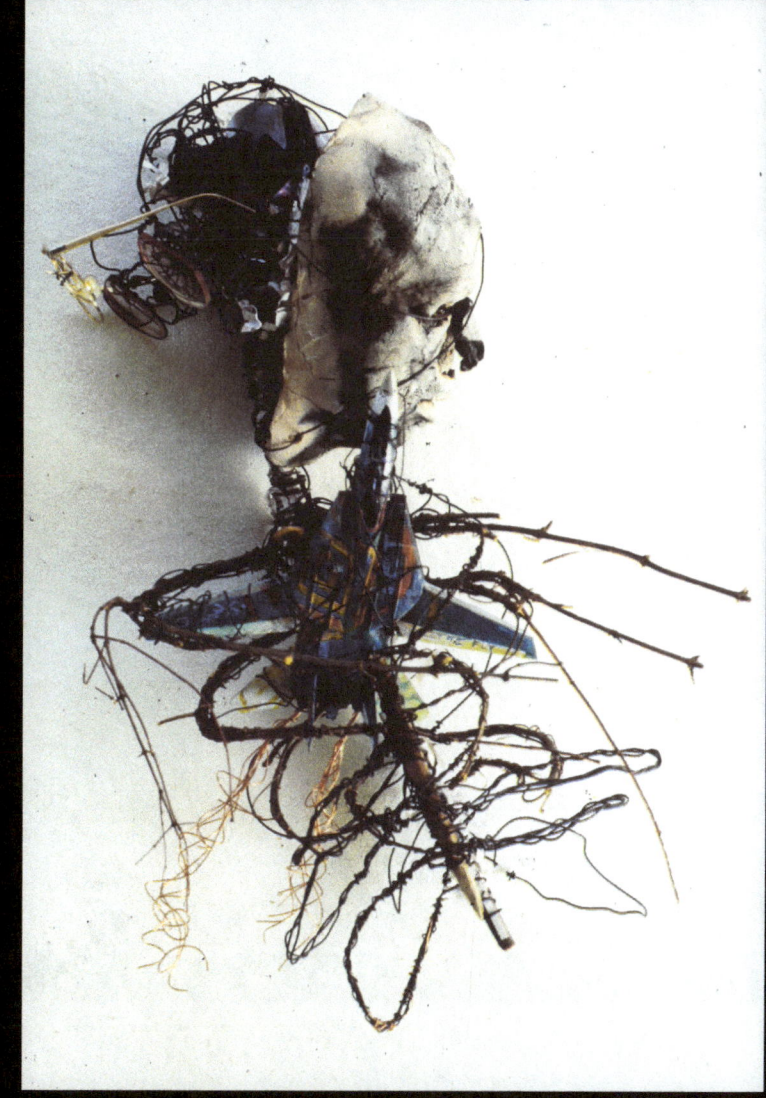

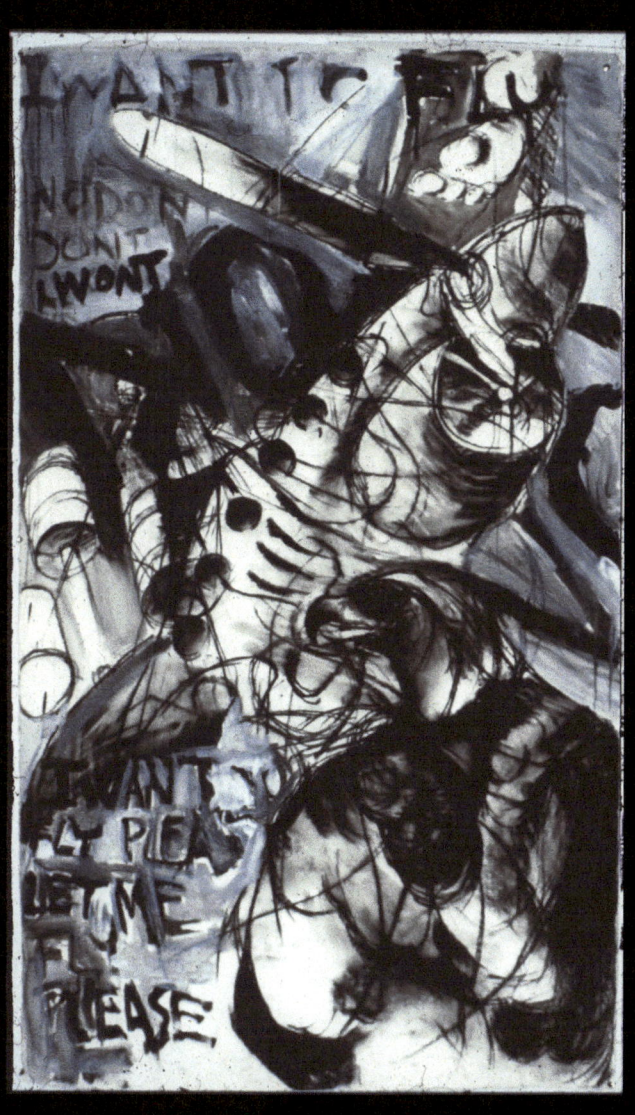

Let Me Fly,
mixed media

Let Me Fly,
1990, mixed media

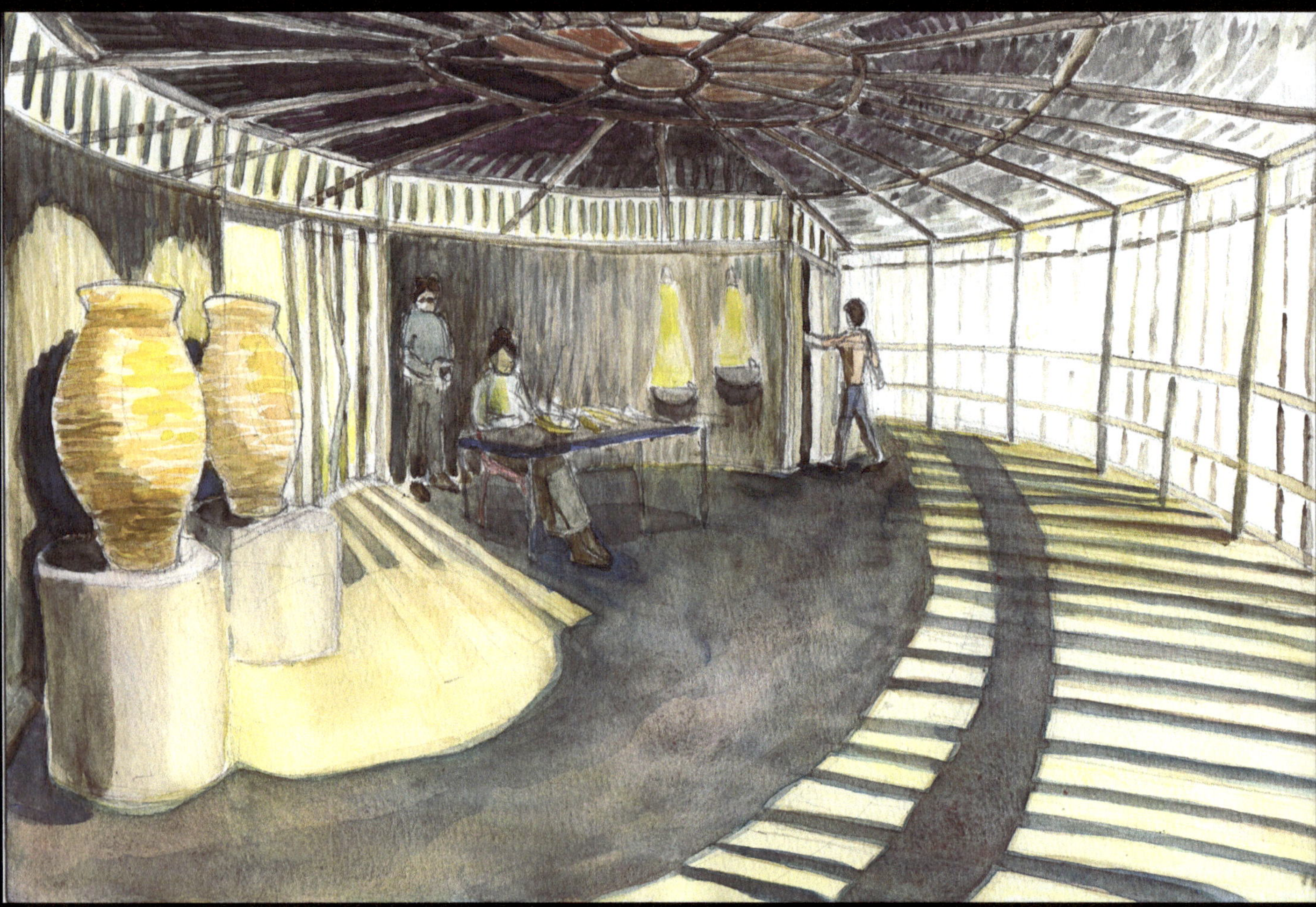

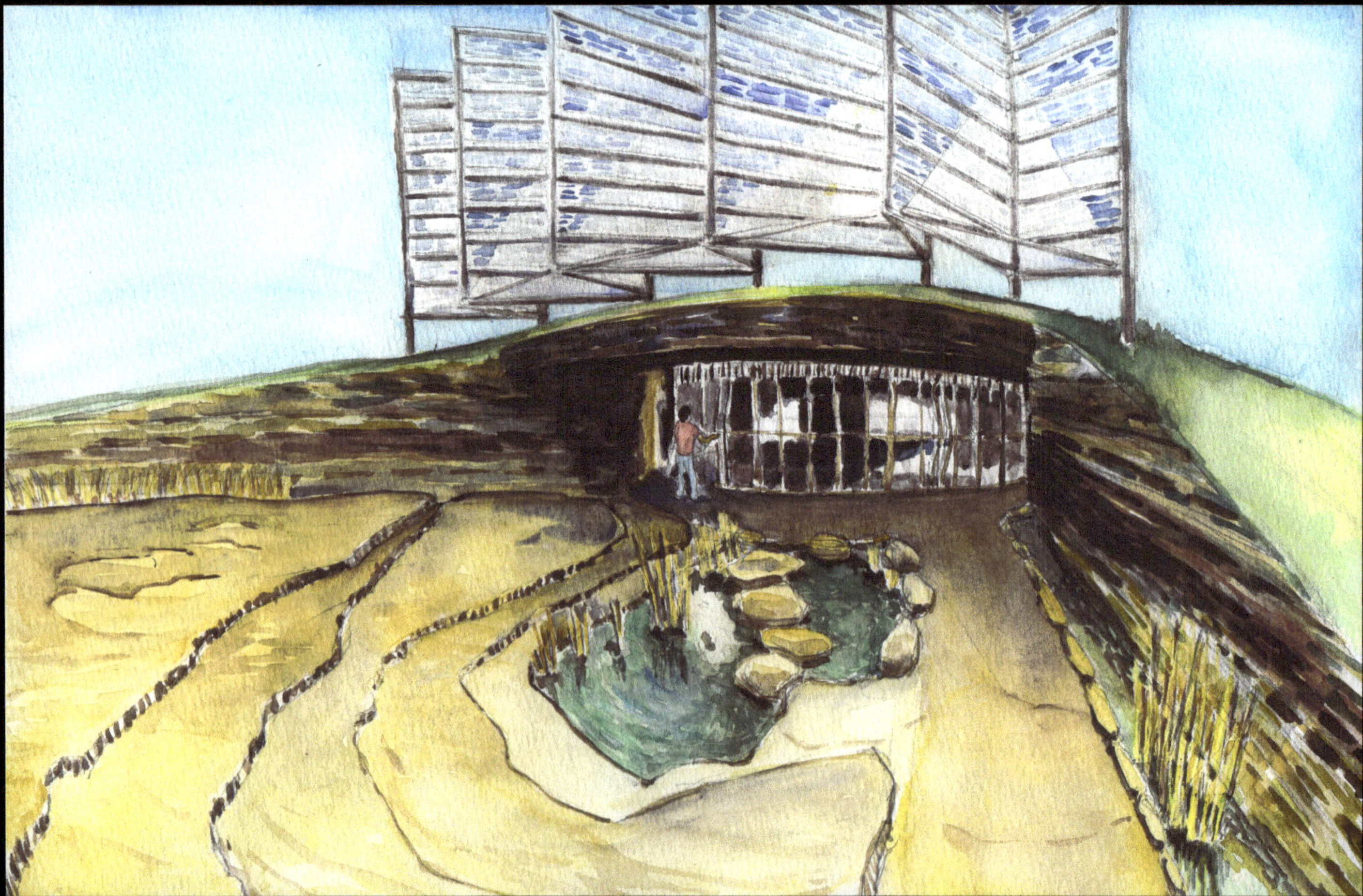

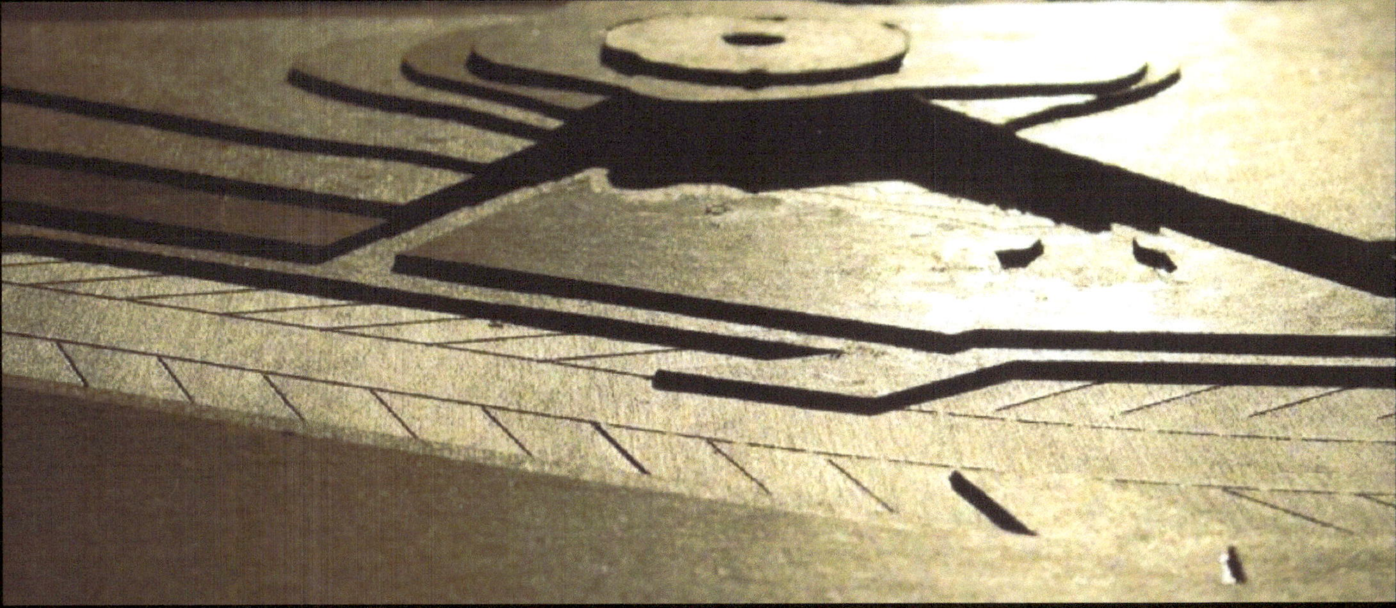

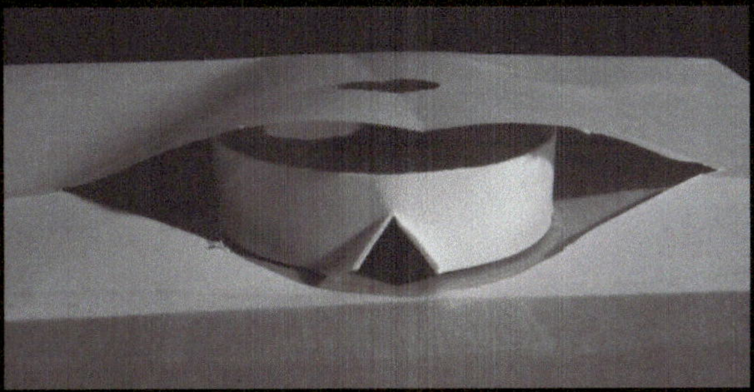

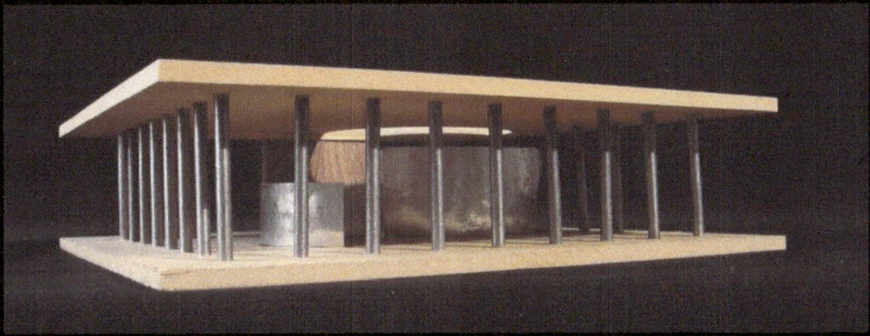

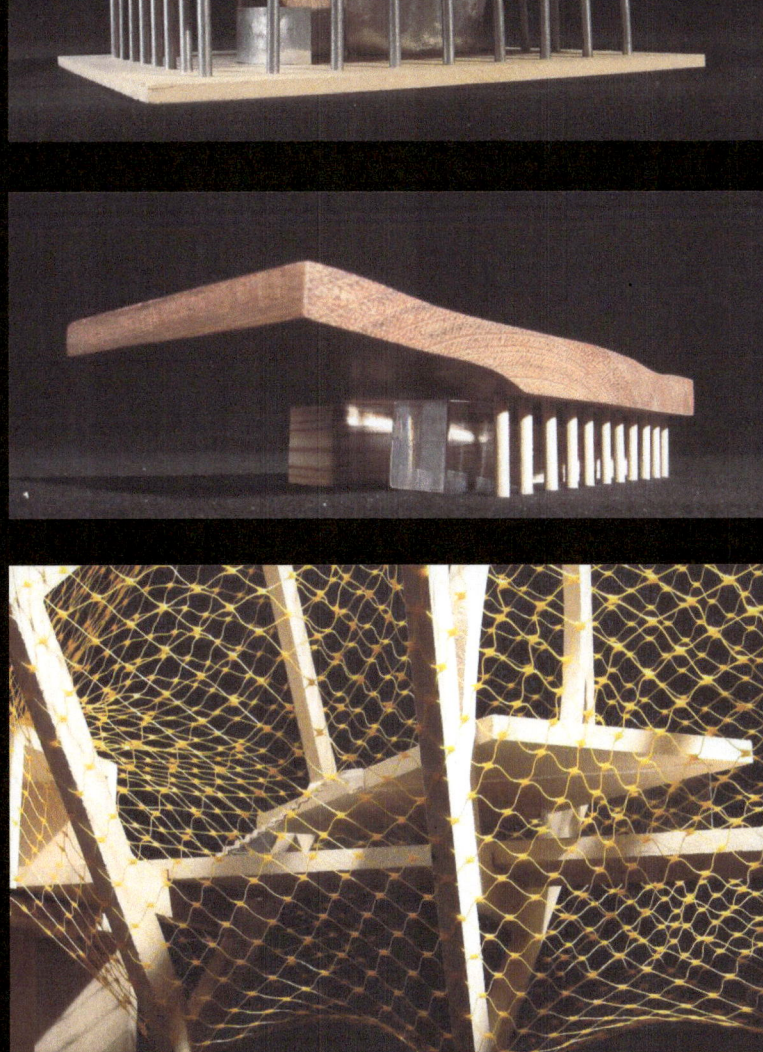

Green Rest Stop,
Illustrations and Models,
2006, watercolor, digital media, cardboard,
paper, wood, steel, plastic, acrylic

These pieces were part of a design proposal
for a rest stop in California. The final idea
was a native building buried underground.
The entryway evokes an archeological dig.
You descend through an excavation into the
historical world of the native peoples of the
area.

The lighting and entry way are inspired by
the Pantheon in Rome combined with traditional lash and pole construction.

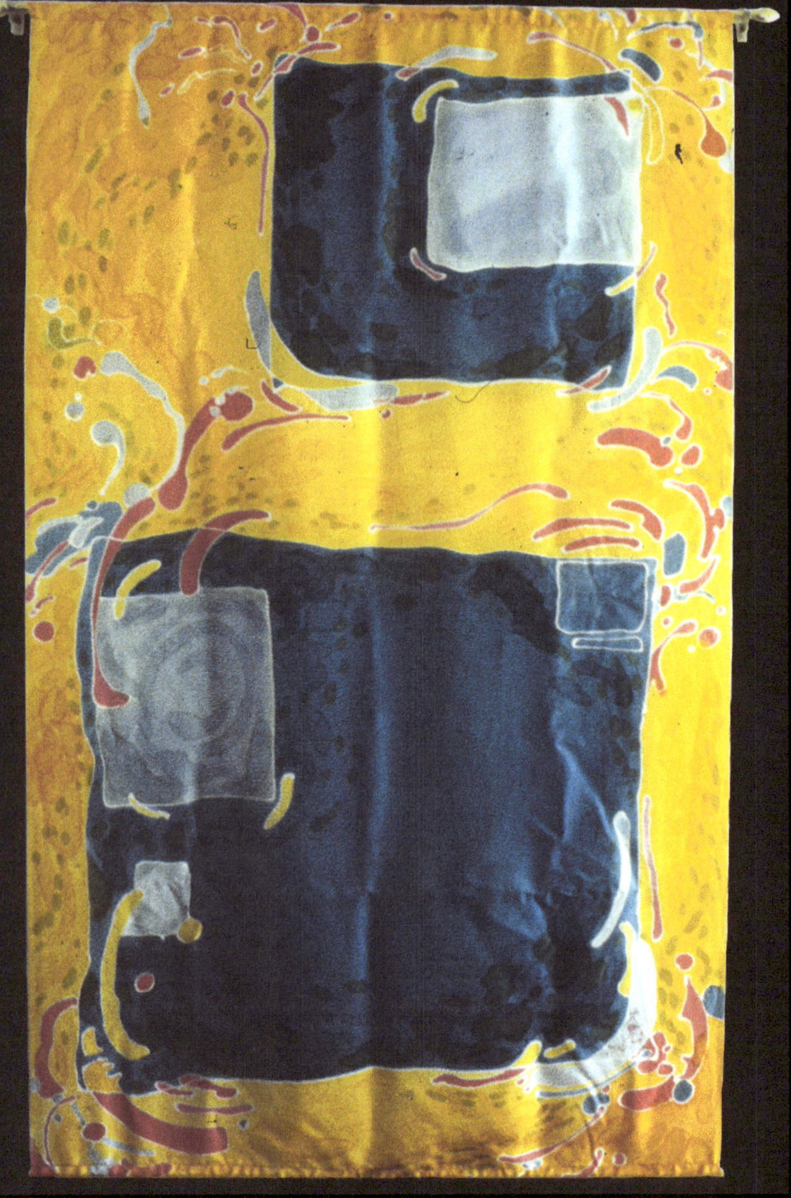

*The Little Pink Dots at the
End of the Universe,*
silk

Grid,
2005, wood, acrylic

Next page:

4 x 4 Grid Section,
2005, wood

This model is pulled from a 4
x 4" section of the grid model
and refers to an outdoor space
as defined in Alexander's
book: *Pattern Language.*

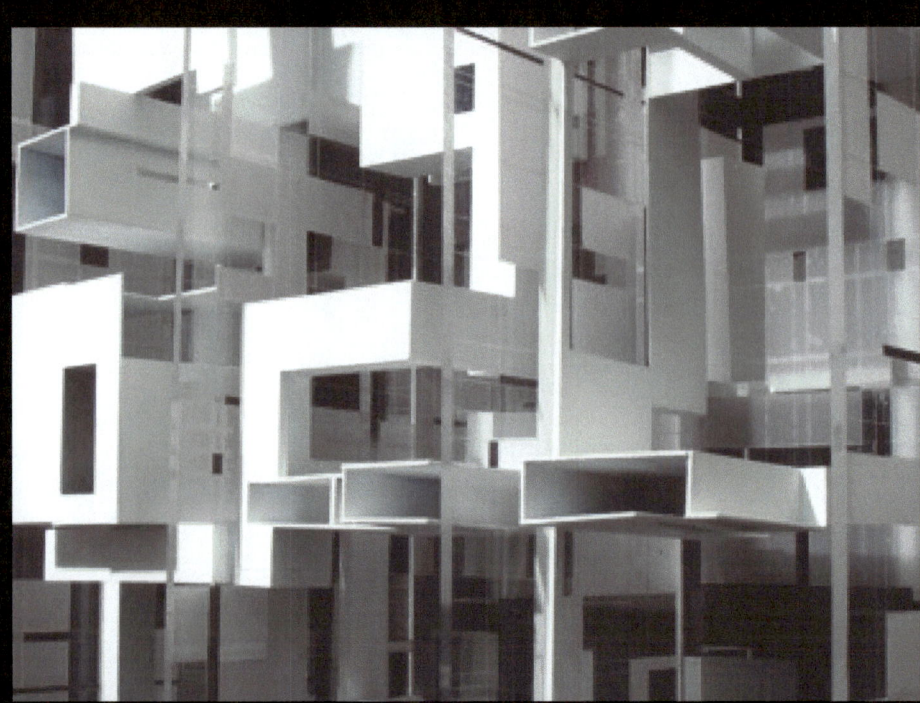

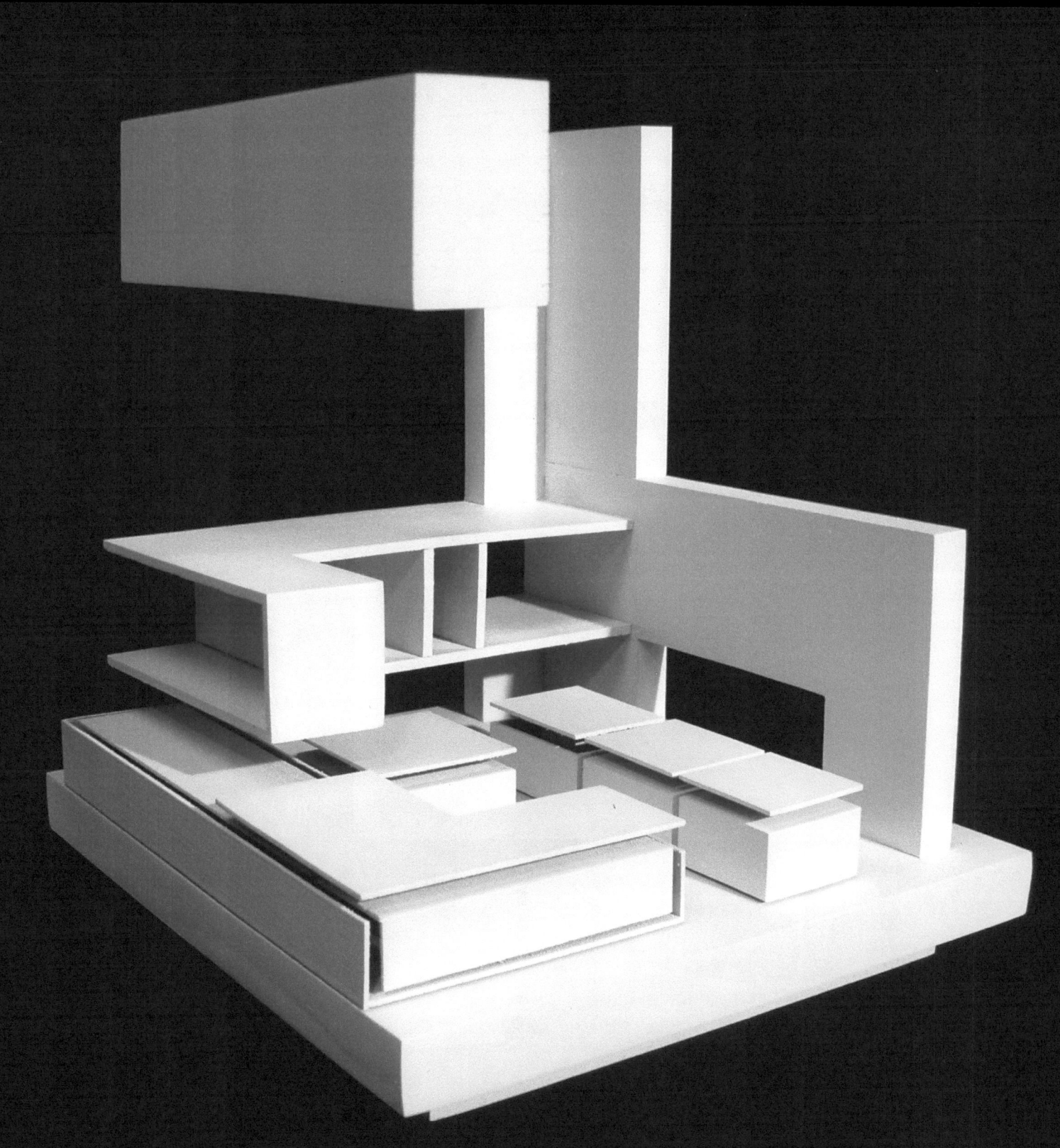

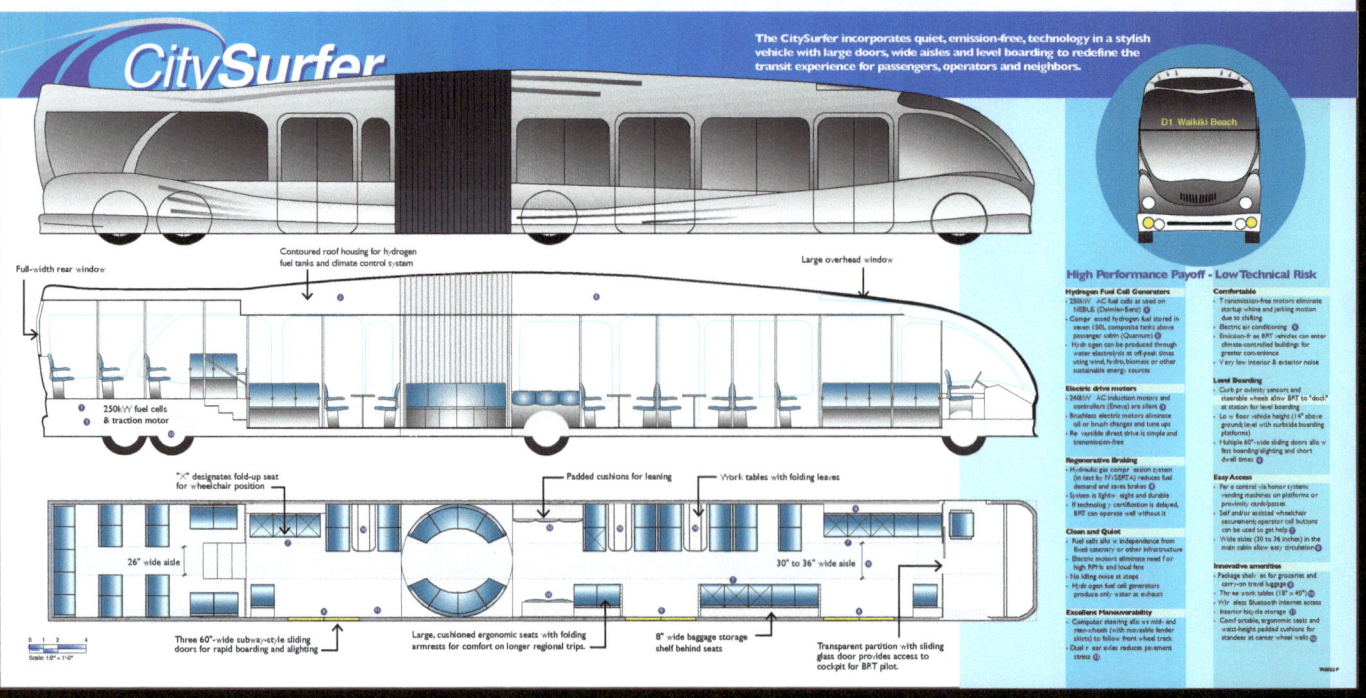

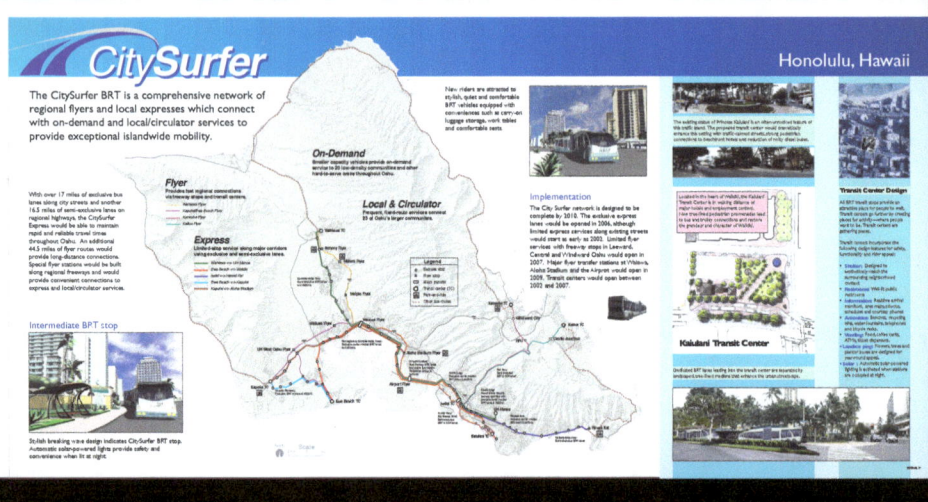

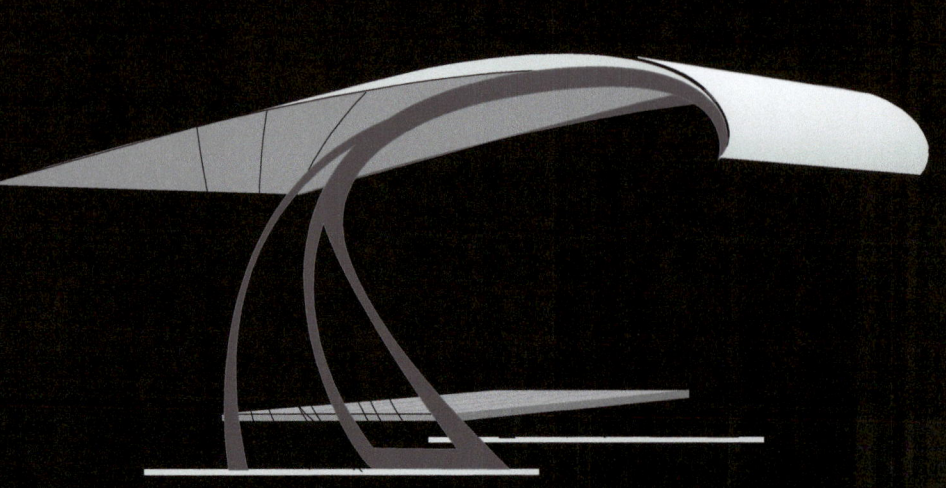

City Surfer BRT, 2002, digital

This proposal by the UH BRT design team won: *Excellence in the Use of Established BRT Concepts, Bus Rapid Transit and the American Community: The National Competition, BRT Consortium*
The UH Design Team developed plans for a BRT system that included routes, stations, vehicles, infrastructure, and social change.

I designed the BRT exterior and the small shelters. The shelter, reflected in the form of the rear window mullion, inspired the logo and name of the submission. Others contributed the 3-D mock-up, researched the technology, planed the route, and created the boards.

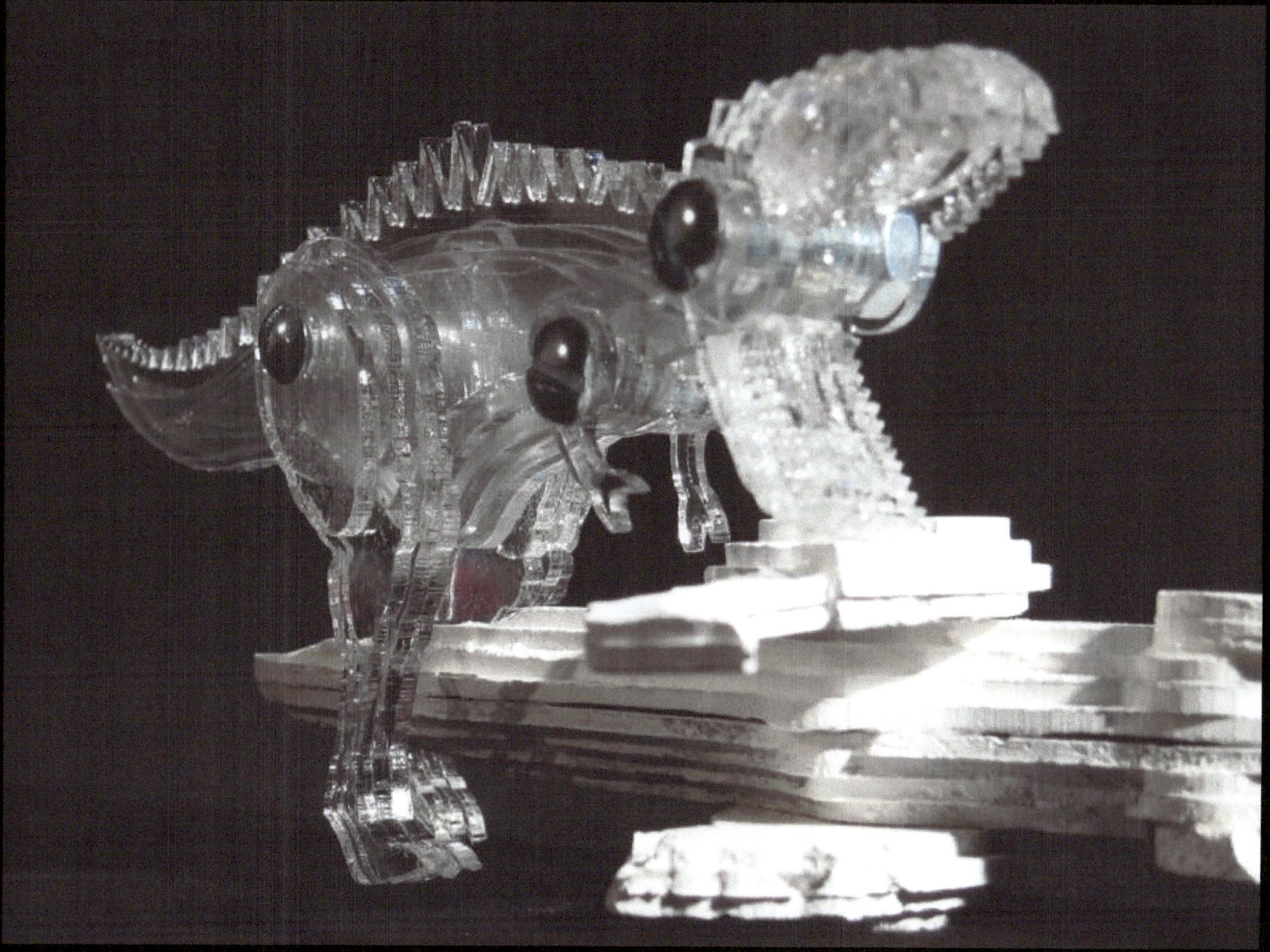

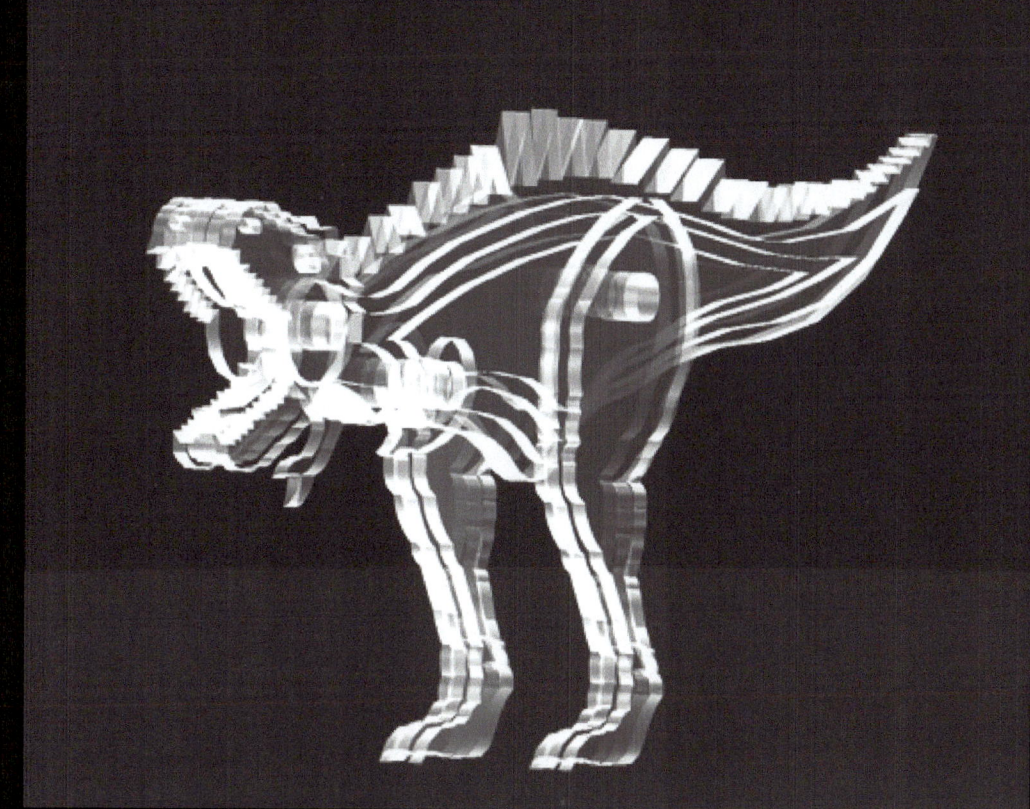

T-Rex,
2006, plexi-glass, plaster

T-Rex,
2006, digital rendering for
the T-Rex toy

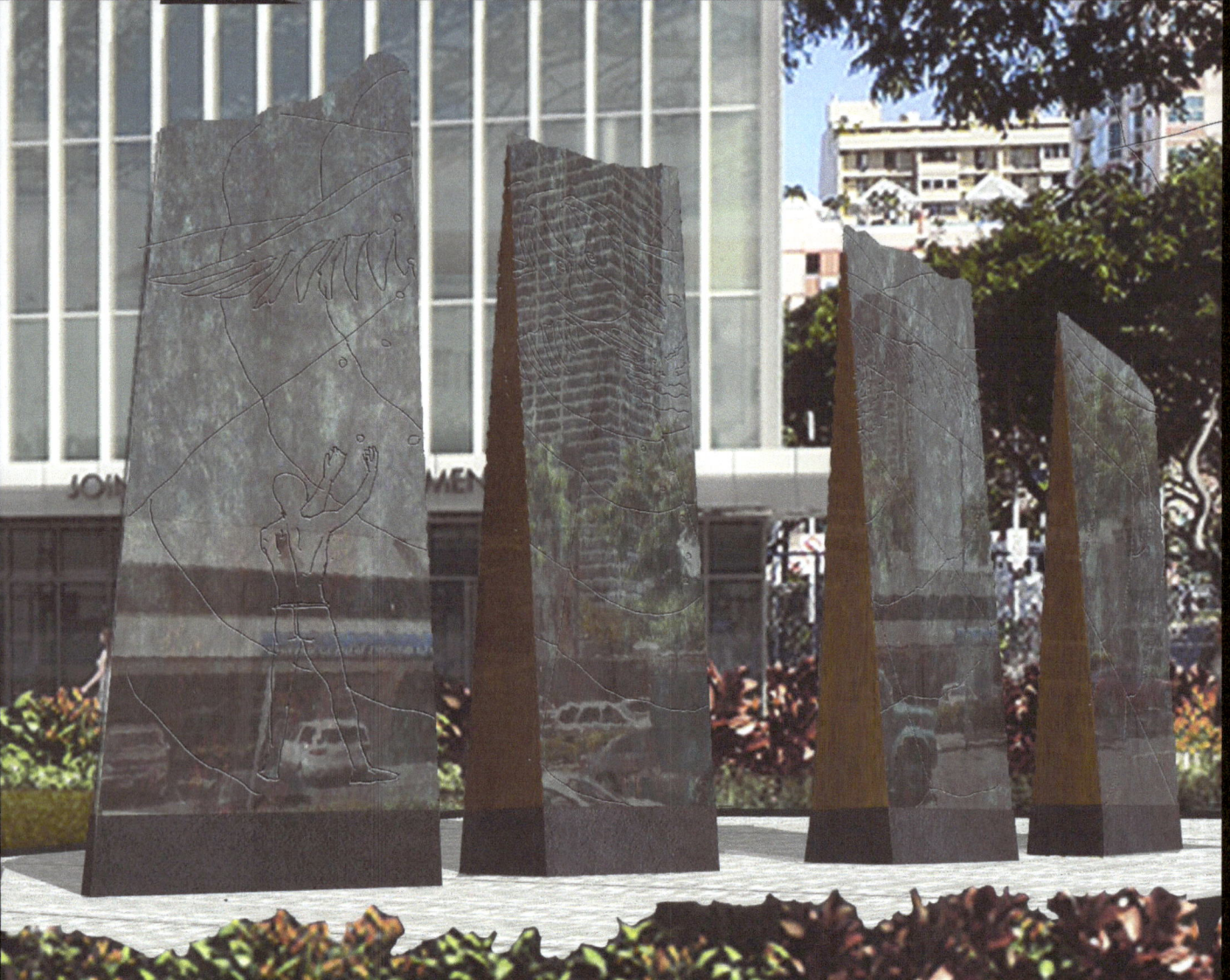

Pu'uowaina (Punchbowl),
2016 digital maquette

The top edge of the sculpture is the ridge line and represents the mo'o's back, spine, and genealogy which is called Kuamo'o. Because the real ridge is now hidden by the city and landscaping, the edge represents the past. Because the surface is reflective you can see yourself in the present.

The cut edges are orange representing Pele. Pu'uowaina is the last place she lived on O'ahu. In one story she freed prisoners of war there.

Etched on the surface is Kapo'i who lived near the present Fort St in Downtown Honolulu in the 1400s. While collecting pili grass on the shore of Kewalo, he found Pueo's (owl) nest. Hungry he took 7 eggs home and prepared them for a meal. Pueo found

him in time and begged for the life of her children. Reluctantly Kapo'i agreed. In the first monolith he is seen returning the 7 eggs to Pueo which ascended into the heavens and became Nāhiku, the Big Dipper. The big dipper directs us to the North Star.

Realizing the power of Pueo, Kapo'i agreed to dedicate a temple to her. Unknowingly, he broke the kapū of the Mo'i. On the far right is a sliver of moon representing the time of Kāne when Kapo'i was supposed to be punished. Pueo (Owl) is blocking the sun as she protects Kapo'i. The sun looks like a spider's web (symbol of the sun and reference to rope and navigation).

The story takes us into the past. The sculpture orients us via its shape, alignment with the stars and by addressing the history of the locality.

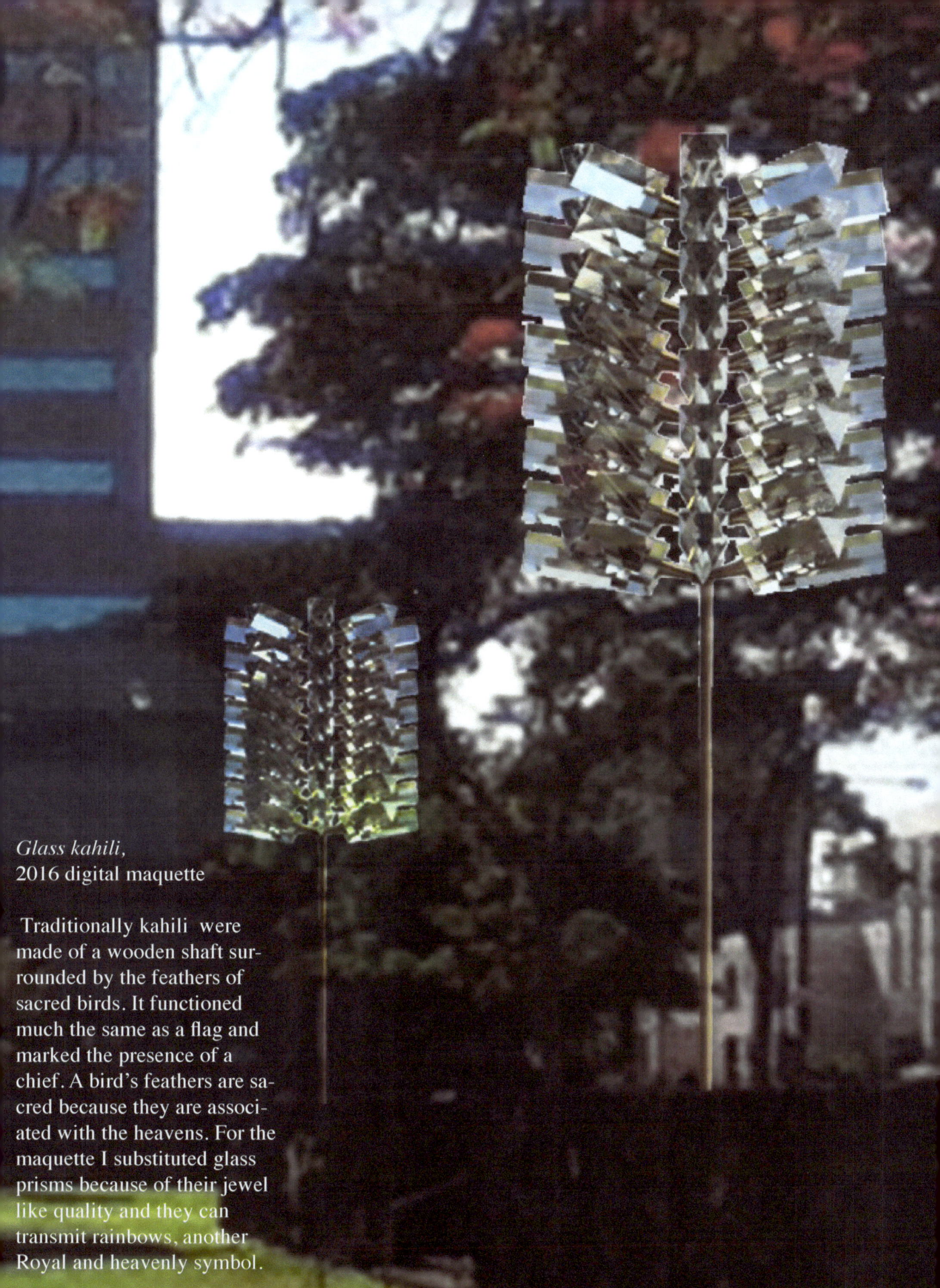

Glass kahili,
2016 digital maquette

 Traditionally kahili were made of a wooden shaft surrounded by the feathers of sacred birds. It functioned much the same as a flag and marked the presence of a chief. A bird's feathers are sacred because they are associated with the heavens. For the maquette I substituted glass prisms because of their jewel like quality and they can transmit rainbows, another Royal and heavenly symbol.

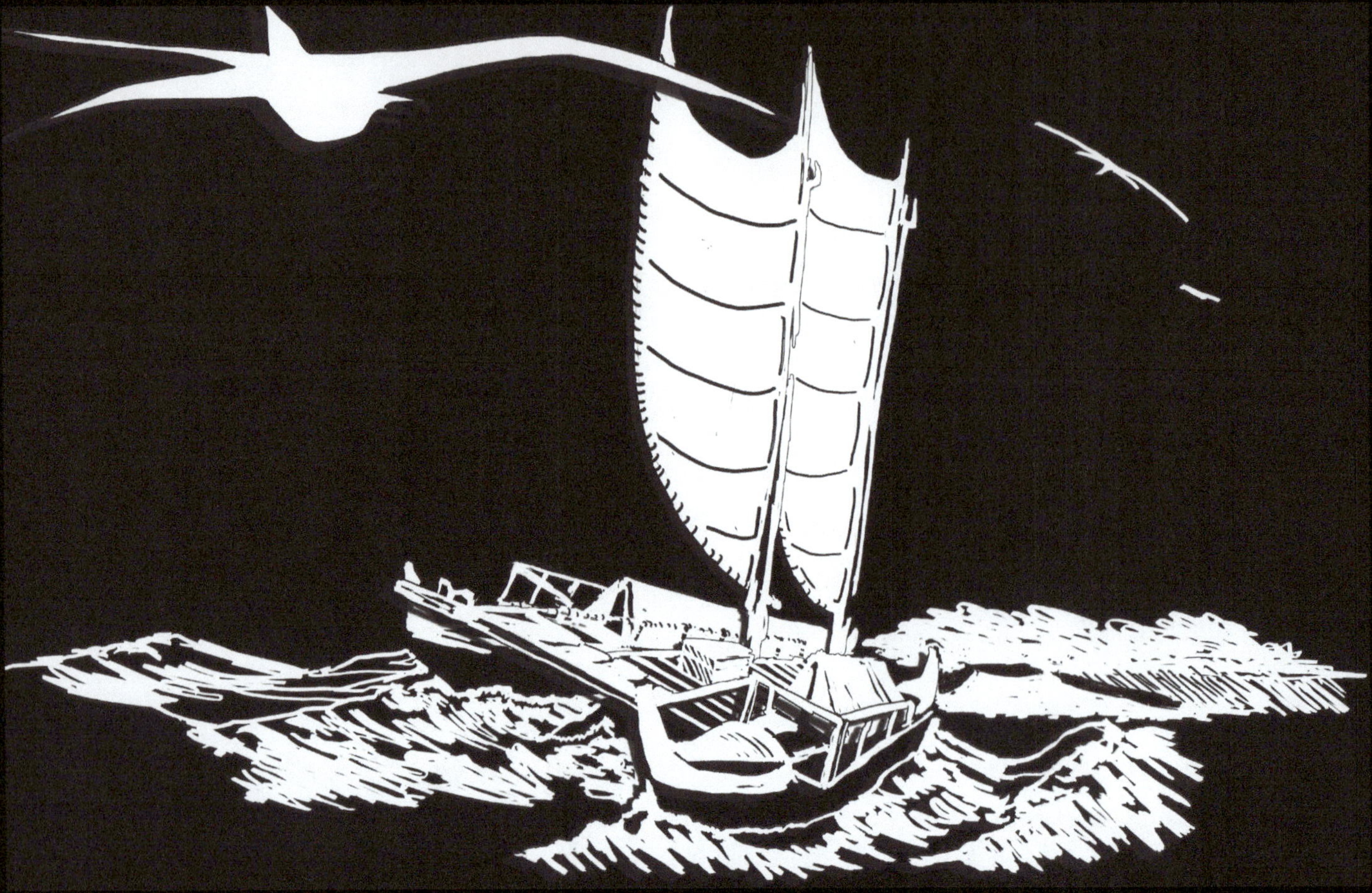

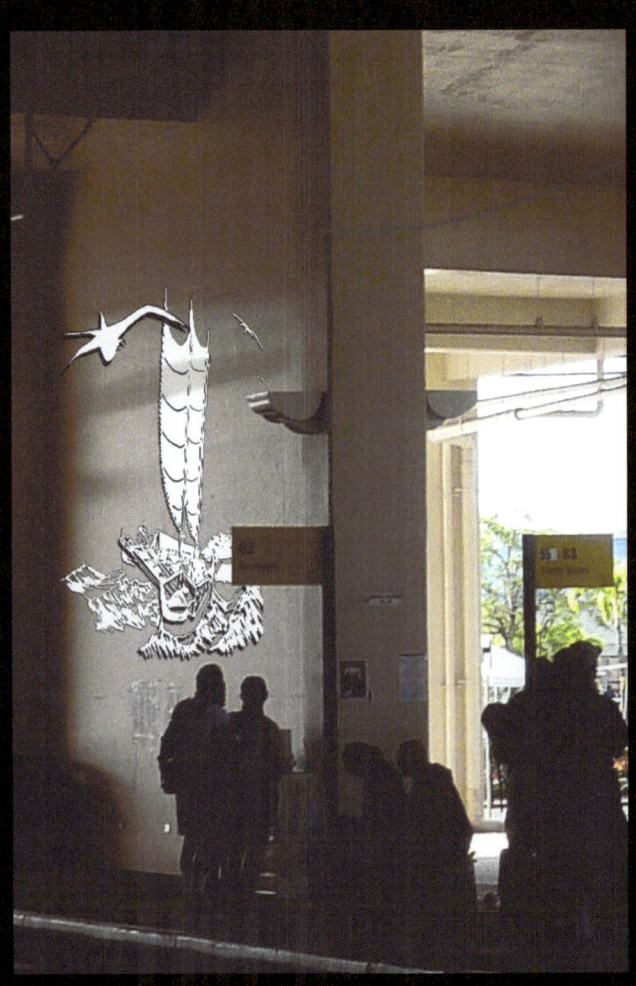

Hōkūleʻa,
2016, digital

 Hōkūleʻa is the modern canoe which helped to inspire
the Renaissance of traditional culture throughout the
Pacific. Hōkūleʻa is translated as *Star of Gladness* and
is named for the star that rises directly over Hawaiʻi.

The ʻIwa or Frigate Bird flying above the canoe is
another sign used by navigators to find land. The pattern of waves and current are used to maintain course.
Changes in the pattern indicates land. The proposed
mural is made of a series of metallic sheets standing off
from a wall.

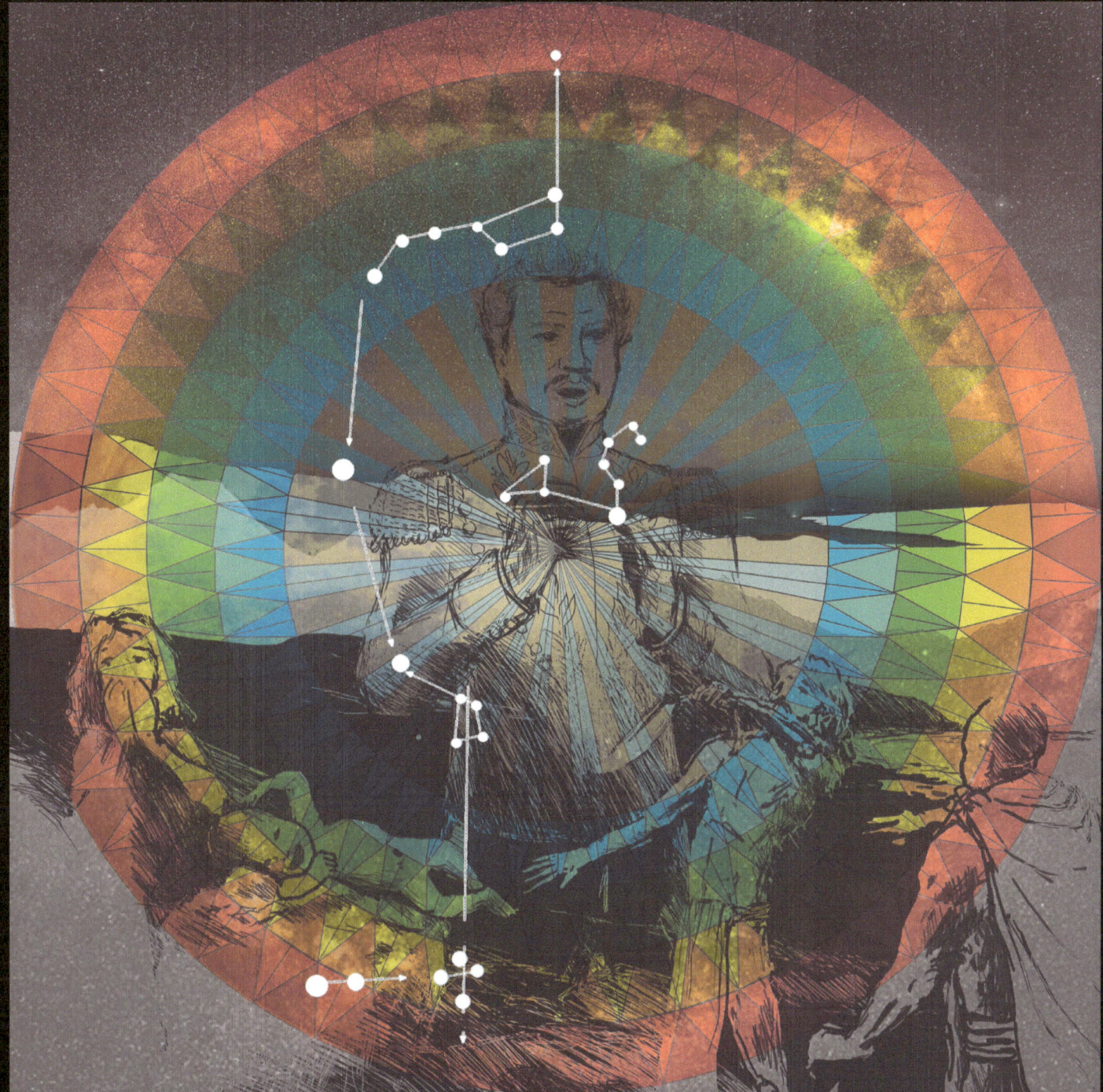

Study for Kauikeaouli's birth,
2016, digital

In the background is the Milky Way as seen from Maunakea representing the time of Kauikeaouli's birth. On the bottom is the Milky Way as seen from New Zealand which reinforces the relationship between Polynesians. Behind the King is Keahou where he was born. On the bottom he is seen as a stillborn baby with his distraught mother. On the right is Kaikioewa who brought the Kaula Kapihe who knows there is life in the child. As Kapihe chants the baby that would be King breathes. Kaikioewa becomes the Prince's Kahu or care taker. The rainbow, star line, and Milky Way are all symbols of the divinity of Kauikeaouli's birth which occurred in a time of year when the bridge between Earth and Heaven is strongest. I referenced a portrait that was done around the time of the incident with the British Consul's takeover of the Kingdom. Admiral Thomas, on orders from the Queen of England, rebuked the Consul and returned power to the King. In the center, Kauikeaouli is addressing the crowd at Thomas Square during the reaffirmation of Hawaiian sovereignty.

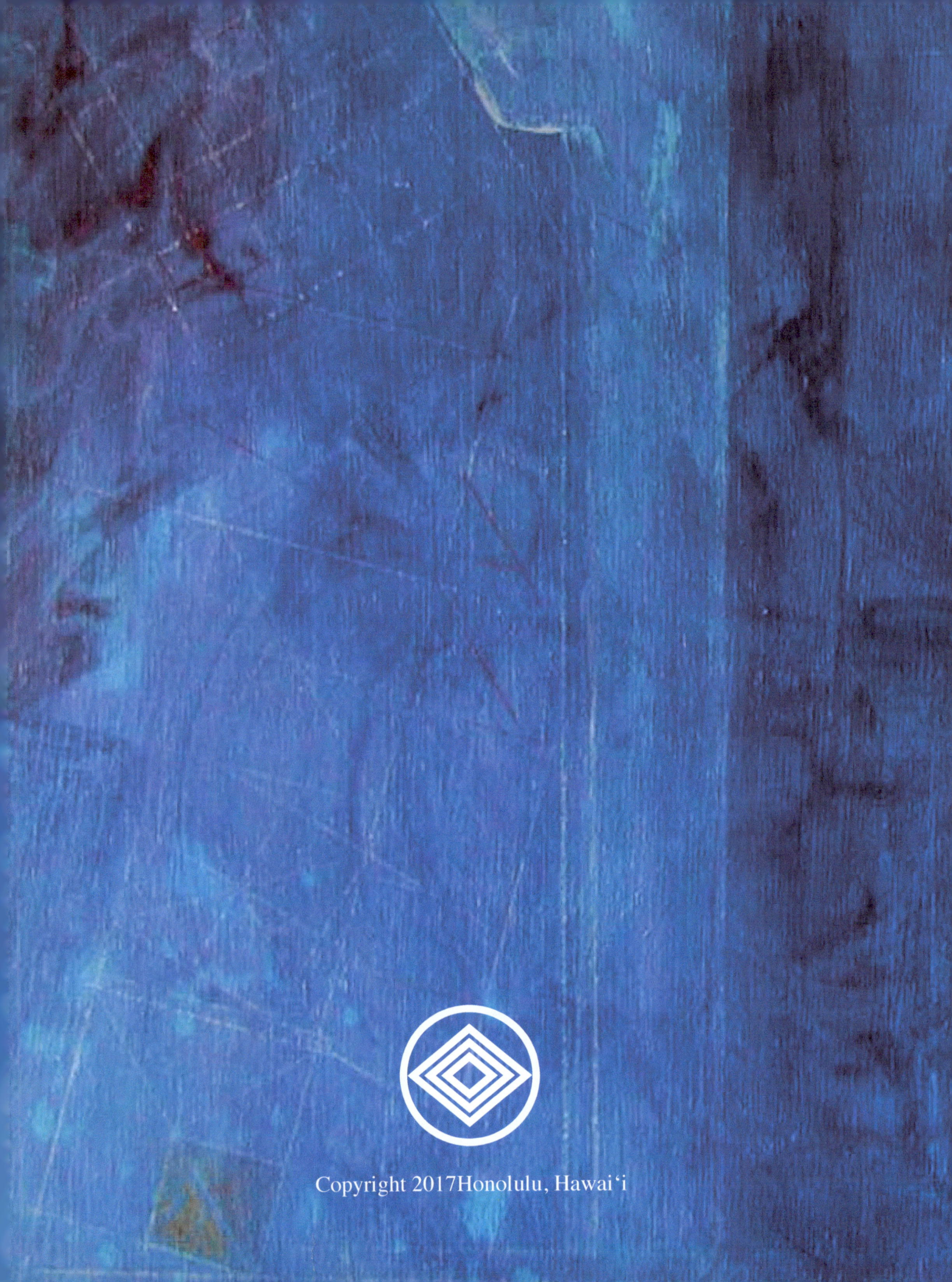

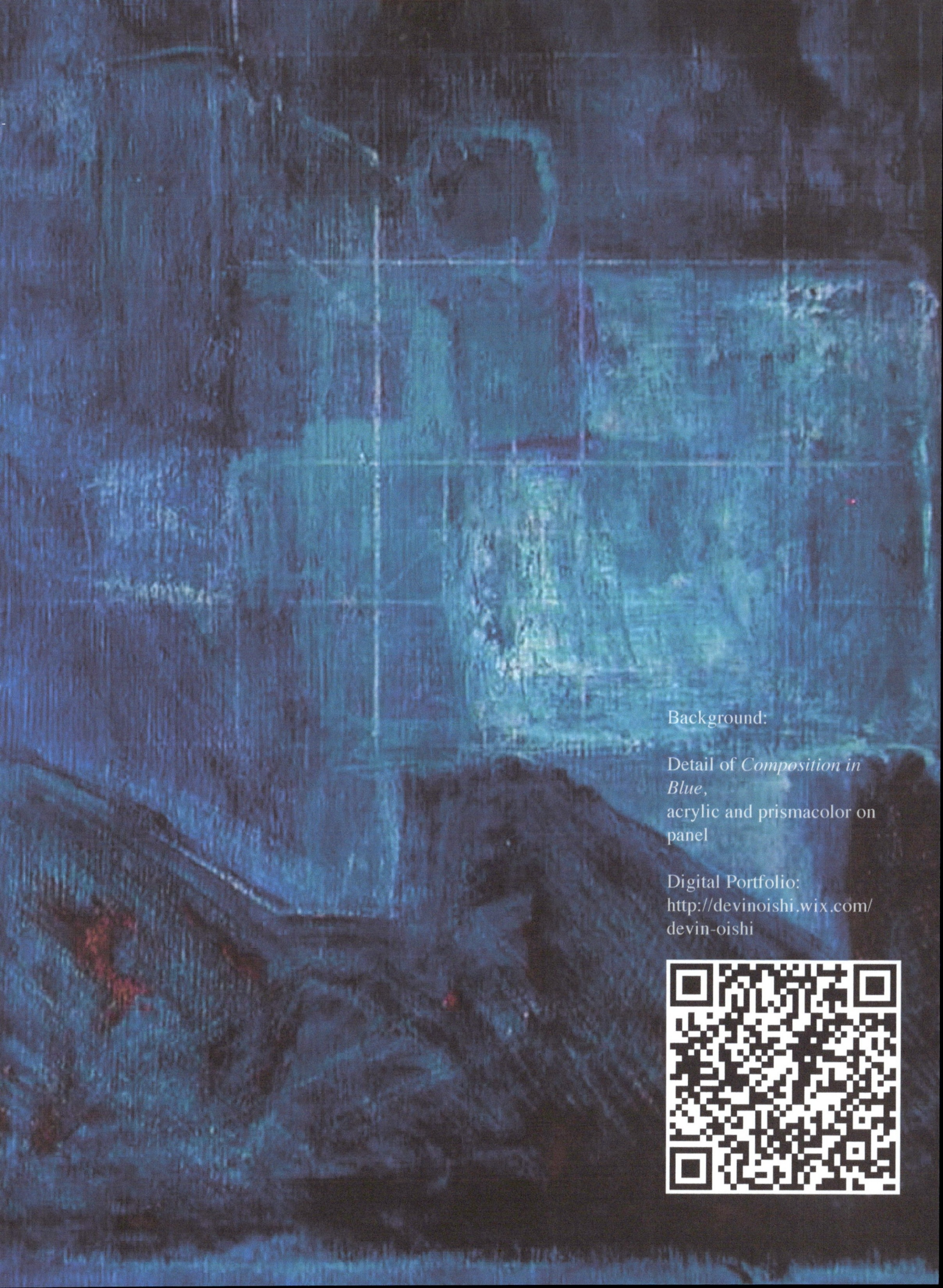

Background:

Detail of *Composition in Blue*,
acrylic and prismacolor on
panel

Digital Portfolio:
http://devinoishi.wix.com/
devin-oishi

www.ingramcontent.com/pod-product-compliance
Lightning Source LLC
Chambersburg PA
CBHW050834180526
45159CB00004B/1896